HOW TO ADVERTISE
AND PROMOTE YOUR
SMALL BUSINESS

"Straightforward and complete, a how-to book
in the best sense of the word.... It presents a
complete survey of advertising methods and
media and gives clear and specific directions
...meant to help businesses use smallness to
their advertising advantage."

—*In Business*

The Small Business Series

DAVID M. BROWNSTONE, *GENERAL EDITOR*

HOW TO ADVERTISE AND PROMOTE YOUR SMALL BUSINESS

Gonnie McClung Siegel

A HUDSON GROUP BOOK

David M. Brownstone, *General Editor*

JOHN WILEY & SONS

New York • Chichester • Brisbane • Toronto • Singapore

Library of Congress Cataloging in Publication Data

Siegel, Gonnie McClung.
 How to advertise and promote your small business.

 (Wiley small business series)
 "A Hudson Group book."
 1. Advertising. 2. Public relations. I. Title.
HF5823.S535   659.1   77-26842
ISBN 0-471-04032-0

Produced and Designed by Ken Burke & Associates

10

Manufactured in the United States of America

CONTENTS

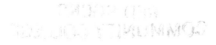

ONE

Introduction

P ROMOTING A SMALL BUSINESS THROUGH ADVERTISING AND publicity is a logical solution to a simple problem—making the buyer aware of the seller.

Approached directly, promotion is simple and easy to apply. It produces results and they can be measured. But if undertaken on the highly technical, mass-marketing basis that the advertising and publicity industry has developed over the last half-century, promotion can swamp a small business in hopelessly complicated procedures.

Goethe, a famous philosopher, could have been talking about promoting a small business when he said, "Everything is simpler than you think, but more complicated than you can imagine."

The small business owner who becomes too deeply enmeshed in the communications business is like the country-and-western singer who decides to study opera. Success in one is likely to reduce success in the other until mediocrity is achieved in both—hardly a desired goal for the small business owner.

You needn't become a communications expert in order to be effective in promoting your business. You should know enough about promotion, however, to know how to use those tools that can help your business. It's impossible to make a judgment about what you need until you know what is available. At their core, a small grocery and General Motors are identical. They

1

both need customers. But the scope of each business and the skills required for successful promotion are vastly different.

Information from hundreds of sources is condensed in this book into a simple guide designed to help you pay next month's rent.

Advertising and public relations are legitimate businesses which produce results, despite persistent rumors that the Madison Avenue/PR world is filled with fools and phonies who couldn't earn an honest living if they tried. (There are some, but probably no more than you'll find in any other business.) Proof of success is that companies invest millions of dollars each year in advertising and public relations and keep coming back for more of this kind of promotion.

What is public relations? Public relations can be defined as press agentry with a college education. A simple matter fifty years ago, public relations now encompasses everything from a brief press release to internal and external communications, image, and public policy in large corporations. It has, as Goethe warned, become more complicated than you can imagine.

Advertising is slightly less complicated, incorporating all forms of paid promotion—from a small public-service announcement to a national advertising campaign involving all types of media and costing millions of dollars. Advertising and public relations are lumped together in large corporations and called "Communications."

For the purposes of the small business owner, promotion is the term most descriptive and most inclusive of everything you'll need. Promotion can be accomplished through paid advertising, such as a newspaper ad or a sign on the back of a bus. Or promotion can be accomplished through publicity, generally free, such as a newspaper article about your business, a speech you make to the local Chamber of Commerce, your name on a homemade poster, or a talking parrot in your store which has attained local fame.

Promotion—whether paid or free—is limited only by your imagination and your sense of what will and won't work. As one public relations executive said, "Good business is putting your best foot forward, but good promotion is making sure a photographer is present when you do it."

As a small business owner, your goal through advertising and publicity should be:

- To communicate clearly with people in order that they understand *exactly* what you mean.
- To communicate with people in a way that will make them *respond* to your communication.

Sound simple? It is simple. Promoting your business will remain simple as long as you keep in mind your clearly defined business objectives and how they can be achieved through realistic promotion. Your overall objective, naturally, is to succeed in business. The ringing of the cash register will tell you whether you've made it.

In promoting your business, always be alert to fresh ideas and new possibilities—but in deciding what type of promotion to try, allow your inner voice to guide you as much as your head. If a wee, small voice awakens you in the night and warns against a clever stunt, give in to your feelings. Unless it *feels* right, it won't *be* right.

So, is this the way Henry Ford, Maxwell House, Tom Watson's IBM, the A&P, Frank Perdue, and the Kentucky Colonel got started?

You bet it is. All the giants began as midgets. Now that they are big they must live with terminal giant disease—a fear that a small budding entrepreneur is building a better mousetrap and cleverly promoting it past them.

Somewhere, some way, some day, someone is struggling to build a small business that will become a multinational corporation, spurred on by the knowledge that the international headquarters of both Reader's Digest and Xerox used to be in garages.

The free-enterprise system is built on a million shoestrings, fueled by human motivation and nourished by dreams. Horatio Alger is alive and well and thinking up clever promotions for a small business.

Anybody who doubts this should take a trip to Plains, Georgia, home of a former small businessman.

TWO

Beginning to Promote Your Business

Time Is Where You Begin / Analyze Your Customers'
Needs / Your Marketing Area / Be a Grower

"THE WISE MAN SAITH, 'PUT ALL YOUR EGGS INTO ONE basket, and watch that basket!'"—Mark Twain in *Pudd'nhead Wilson.*

- You've put all your eggs into one small business, and every other night you dream of vast success. On alternate nights, you dream of meeting next month's bills and of being able to afford part-time help to sweep up the floor.
- You've established a small business which has been moderately successful over the past few years, but in the back of your head lingers a nagging thought that you must be doing something wrong, or your business would be doing much better.
- You've recently set up a new business. It took off like a bird those first few weeks, but now it's leveled off and profits are much lower than your original expectations. Are you doing something wrong, or were your early expectations unrealistic?

Whatever your circumstances, is a big advertising and publicity campaign the medicine your business needs to really soar?

Can a marginal business be kept afloat indefinitely through clever promotion? Everybody has heard stories about bad products sold through good advertising. Everybody knows that the way to get people to eat Crunchy Crispies instead of Crispy Crunchies is to sell hard through advertising. Does the same hold true in a small business?

Emphatically no! Clever promotion alone cannot keep you in business, no matter how original your advertising and publicity. And a mass-marketing approach—such as in selling breakfast cereals—wouldn't help a small local business if it were free. If your business is in Ohio, do you really need to reach people in Vermont? Promoting your business outside your marketing area is a waste of time, energy, and money.

Promotion is, however, a very important piece of your business success puzzle. Used effectively, it can produce dramatic results that may overshadow other, equally important, success factors.

For example, when a small business doubles its profits after a promotional campaign, it's only natural to believe the promotion alone did the trick. In analyzing your success, however, you must take into consideration that the product or services advertised were there to begin with. Otherwise you would have had nothing to advertise. The argument that advertising "creates need" will go on as long as the chicken-and-the-egg argument, with the same kind of circular logic. But gold toothpicks are not likely to become a big seller, no matter how much they are promoted. A *potential* need must exist, or the promotion will not succeed. If somebody had tried to sell distilled water a hundred years ago, he or she would have been laughed out of town. A hundred years from now, somebody may be selling bottled air. People who recognize changing needs often give the illusion of creating needs.

No matter where you are located or what kind of business you intend to start, first analyze the need for what you have to offer. However, if there are six drugstores in the same community, the one with the most effective promotion will probably garner the biggest profits, assuming all other factors are equal.

Naturally, if you could lay out $100,000 for a whopping promotional campaign it would help your business. But if you had that kind of money to spend on promotion, you wouldn't be in a small business. If you can scrape together enough money for a quarter-page ad in the local newspaper once a week and print 500 special flyers twice a year, you're in tune with thousands of small businesses dotting the landscape from Maine to California.

"It's unusual to find an adequately capitalized small business," says a former official of the Small Business Administration. "Most people go into business on a shoestring, and boom or bust on sheer energy and guts. Sometimes energy and guts are enough, but it's a risky substitute for capital."

"The definition of a small business," says the owner of a wholesale paper-goods firm, "is work and money. Too much of one and too little of the other. Every small business owner knows which is which."

"The greatest factor in my going into business," says the owner of a small newspaper, "was ignorance. I'm glad I did it, now that I've made it, but I'd never do it again knowing what I know now."

TIME IS WHERE YOU BEGIN

Now that you've reaffirmed what you already knew—that no small business ever had enough money or enough help—how do you begin to develop a successful promotional strategy? How, exactly, can you pick and choose the *right* advertising and publicity for your business, and execute it in the half-hour a day you feel you have left over after minding the store?

That's the start of your problem: Time. Your time. Every last second of it is the most precious commodity you have in a small business. Every moment can be translated into profit or loss, and too often it is loss. Spending time inefficiently means you're sweeping profits out the front door, out the back door, and down into cracks in the floor.

Analyze your time in order to find the time you'll need to promote your business. For example, while you're trimming the window in your small store, you can be thinking up other promotional ideas. One petshop owner discovered that passersby would stop to watch him work while he was in his display window. So he added a pair of hamsters to his display, complete with a running treadmill. People stopped to look because the live movement attracted their attention. When the hamsters died, the owner replaced them with a parrot which became quite famous in the small town.

"I figured I'd add sound to my window movie," he said. "The parrot was good for starting conversations. People would come into the store to ask me about the parrot, and I'd end up getting their names on my mailing list."

This parrot ended up as an identifying logo on all pamphlets, ads, and direct mailing pieces from the store, providing instant recognition for customers. Although a pet parrot and a petshop were logical connections, many shop owners could do the same thing with the same results. All it takes is a little imaginative promotion.

In analyzing her time, the owner of a beauty shop also took a look at what her customers were doing with theirs. She discovered that many were reading her trade magazines rather than *Glamour* and *Good Housekeeping*. Based on this knowledge, she made up a true-false test about hair care, using technical information such as the chemical contents of hair coloring and which brands of hair spray destroy the ozone layer.

"I discovered that my customers were really interested in learning that some hair coloring contains the same chemicals as oven cleaner," the owner said. "The test worked so well and created so much interest that I ended up using it in an ad in the local newspaper. It brought in many new customers more interested in healthy hair care than in beauty care."

ANALYZE YOUR CUSTOMERS' NEEDS

Before you can decide on what and where to advertise or publicize, you must decide *what* it is that you are selling. If you're selling something that people need or want—either goods or services—you're even with your competition. But just being even is not enough. You must stay ahead. You must figure out what your customers want and what kind of edge you can gain over the competition.

A small grocer, eclipsed by six supermarkets, analyzed his weekly specials, his prime meat department, and his clean, well-stocked shelves, and came up with a small service to add to his competitive edge over the nearby giants. He discovered that many people were running into his store each day for a quart of milk or a loaf of bread, the usual one or two pick-up items which account for sizable traffic in a small grocery. But on their way out, many customers complained of the absence of express lanes in the nearby supermarkets. In response, the alert owner installed a special buzzer to his office. It was located up front near the check-out lanes, with a sign which said: "Ring me if you can't get out."

The sign served two productive purposes. It notified the customer of the added service, and it notified the check-out crew that the boss didn't want to see long lines and slow service. The sign produced compliments from customers and knocks for the competition. So on a weekly newspaper ad and in direct mailing flyers, the owner added a bottom line: "Supermarkets rope you in but they won't let you out. *We have the fastest express lane in town!*" The ad hit a responsive chord in the big supermarkets' customers, and the store owner hit on a hidden competitive edge.

YOUR MARKETING AREA

Most small business owners can draw a circle on a map that will include 99 percent of their marketing area. But within your marketing circle there are many different groups, all potential customers. Often the larger group is dominated by a smaller specific group.

It's logical that a small business in a retirement village cater to the special needs of older people. The same kind of logic applies to businesses in resort areas or ethnic neighborhoods. Focusing special attention on race, color, age, sex, religion, occupation, place of origin, or marital status may be discrimination in a large business—but it's good marketing in a small business. Within all the different groups included in your marketing area, carefully study your prospective customers' needs with an eye toward providing a unique or special service, and promoting it. A service station may offer special services to taxicab owners. A hardware store may offer power tools for rent to nearby apartment-dwellers who haven't the space to store their own.

One auto repair shop owner caters to commuters who go to the train station near his business. A customer who brings in a car in the morning gets a free ride to the station. The car is repaired during the day and the commuter is picked up in the evening. You can bet the owner's promotional efforts stress this unique commuter service.

Shakespeare might have said, "All the world's a store, and all the people in it merely customers." Whether they will become *your* customers depends upon what you do to:

- Recognize a need.
- Provide a service.
- Promote your service.

A few years ago, a government-sponsored study compared businesses in five cities in order to learn what makes a business grow. Here are some of the reasons behind growth and success:

- Those who liked their business best tended to grow the most.
- The growers tried to serve their customers instead of serving themselves.
- The rapid growers took less money out of their businesses in the early stages. They also spent more hours working.
- Growers became good managers in *all* phases of their businesses.
- The growers could identify more problems, but could also come up with more solutions.
- The growers constantly asked advice, free and paid, took the advice seriously, and applied it to their businesses.

BE A GROWER

Once you've figured out your marketing area, your strong points, and your competitive edge, stand back and look objectively at yourself and your business. Chances are you'll pick out the right things on which to hinge your promotional campaign. Start slowly and build steadily. If you have correctly analyzed your customers' needs and you are ready to provide a better solution to those needs than anyone else is providing, there's only one thing left to do in order to become a grower: Tell your customers and potential customers what you're doing.

Call it advertising, public relations, communications, publicity, community relations, promotion, or anything you like. But once you've got the hang of doing it, there's one thing you'll call it for sure. Good business.

THREE

Promotion:
The Sky Is *Not* the Limit

*Planning a Successful Campaign / Where to Begin /
Keeping It Simple / Don't Just Sit There—Do Something*

T HE GOODYEAR BLIMP GLIDES ON ITS PROMOTIONAL WAY
on a clear day, high above the tall buildings. An airplane
streaks out a politician's message—promotion by skywriting. A
daily newspaper article features a lion-tamer who puts two huge
cats through their paces in a downtown department store; a cir-
cus benefit performance is being underwritten by the store—a
promotional stunt.

Authors and actors parade on and off a late-evening television
talk show, promoting their books, plays, and movies. Two
teams of youngsters announce a price war in competing lemon-
ade stands outside their homes; they are interviewed by a local
radio station.

It's all *promotion.* Everywhere you look, somebody is selling
something through promotion—directly or indirectly. Part of
every newspaper is filled by press releases or stories about events
planned to promote a person, product, or service. Much of television entertainment is outright promotion. Movie stars horse-
trade appearances for exposure of their movies. A high federal
official is interviewed by Johnny Carson in order to promote a
special government program. Even the President calls a press
conference in order to "go directly to the people," which means
that he's promoting something.

Promotion can be good or bad—good for your business or
bad, depending upon the kind of promotion. Keep in mind that

promotion for its own sake is easy and useless. You are guaranteed a front-page slot on most of the nation's newspapers, plus network television and radio coverage, if you climb a flagpole on Christmas Day and sit there nude, playing a banjo. Except for unusual circumstances, however, this kind of promotion won't sell anything—not even banjos, nudity, or flagpoles. In fact such promotion, if you were foolish enough to do it, might help put you out of business.

Successful promotion for a small business should be carefully selected for specific results. It must do one or more of the following:

- Get favorable attention.
- Create an interest in your business.
- Stimulate customer action.
- Increase your profits directly or indirectly.

When you begin a promotional idea, first write down everything you plan to do that will further your business goals—exactly how the promotion will increase your sales. Many ideas that seem terrific, on first glance, don't stand up well when written down and analyzed for every possible angle—good or bad. After you write down your ideas, allow a little time between the thought and the action. Last week's great idea may turn out, after consideration, to be this week's worst bet.

Keep your notes about any promotional campaign, and file them away so that you can go over them later and figure out why some succeeded and others didn't. That way you'll know which ones to repeat and which to put in your dead file, chalked up to the learning process.

Don't expect promotion to work out perfectly every time. It won't. Some ideas lie there limp, never getting off the ground. Others, that you thought were only so-so, take off and fly to unexpected success. The important thing to remember is to analyze everything and *never, never* make the same mistake twice.

PLANNING A SUCCESSFUL CAMPAIGN

There is no guarantee of success when you enter the world of promotion, whether you are a beginner or a professional. The professional, through experience, is better able to maximize the possibility of success and minimize the causes of failure. He or she knows what will work and what will bomb, generally, but not always.

When a professional plans an outdoor event, the weather is automatically considered an important element in the planning process. Alternatives are standard procedure. The amateur might plan a similar event without considering the weather at all. Weeks of hard work could be destroyed because of a half-hour rainstorm. This kind of disaster happens over and over again to those inexperienced in the promotion business: a whistling microphone ruins a speech; a creaking door ruins a meeting; rain ruins a picnic.

For example, a small manufacturer in the Midwest decided to sponsor a tour through his plant—a good, practical promotional idea that has worked for many people many times. The manufacturer bought a small ad in his hometown newspaper, inviting the townspeople; he called up the mayor and members of the city council and asked them to be guests of honor. He then bought champagne, hired a marching band, and stationed guides throughout the plant to squire around the expected mob attendance. Fewer than 50 people showed up, and about a fourth of these were the special guests—those who had been given a special reason for attending.

The owner made a common mistake. He took for granted that the townspeople and his own employees were as interested in his business as he was. But they weren't as interested. They needed to be sold—to be given an incentive for showing up. Plant employees didn't want to rush back to their place of employment on a Sunday afternoon, and the townspeople hadn't been motivated to attend.

With the right kind of promotion, the plant owner's goal of a full house could easily have been met. He could have sent a simply worded invitation to his own employees, asking them to bring their families to an open-house tour. He could have told them and mentioned in the newspaper ad that the high school marching band would perform and that champagne would be served. He could have listed some interesting things about the plant's history and explained some things that would be featured in the tour.

In carefully planned promotion, one piece builds on the next and produces a pyramid effect. A person who reads an ad about an event will be more likely to read an article about it, or vice versa. Familiarity breeds interest. An individual who reads both an ad and an article will be more likely to listen to a radio program about the event, or read a poster or respond to an invitation or talk to the neighbors about it. Each bit of promotion builds interest before, during, and after the event and can continue far into the future.

WHERE TO BEGIN

In planning a successful promotion, begin not at the beginning but at the end—your goal is always where you should start. By beginning with your objective—what you want the promotion to accomplish—you can test every idea against the goal. Unless it furthers your goal, discard it. Beginning with your objective keeps your eye on the target and discourages a shotgun approach.

Suppose your objective is to attract new customers to your place of business. Write on a pad:

- Objective: New customers.
- Various possibilities: The "how" part of the equation.
- Specific possibilities: Narrow your ideas down to a beginning.
- Methods of promotion: Advertising, publicity.
- Specific methods: Flyers, posters, direct mail, ads.
- Budget: Put it down, even if it's only $50.
- Expected results: What you want your efforts to accomplish.
- Measured results: The final accounting. Did it work or not? Why? File away.

Regardless of what you do in the way of promotion, you will attract your regular customers, but attracting them is not your primary objective here. In any promotion to attract new customers, be sure to stress your location—let them know specifically how to find you. Perhaps you can identify your location by a local landmark such as the town hall, a library, a church, a well-known street. Make it as easy as possible for new customers to find you.

Next, you need to motivate and persuade strangers to make their way to your door for the very first time. It may take strong inducement—the stronger the inducement, the better your chances for success. Again, this will also pull in regular customers; but stick to your objective of bringing in new people.

Suppose you own a small restaurant, and you decide that a catchy promotional idea would be to roll back your menu prices to match those of a famous landmark restaurant in 1928. You advertise 1928 prices: coffee, 5¢; apple pie, 10¢; a hamburger, 10¢; breakfast, 25¢; dinner, 90¢. It's a sure bet that you'll pull in almost 100 percent of your regular customers, but you will also draw new customers who may become regulars from that day forward. Whether your promotion is a success or not will depend on how many of them return as a result of that promotion.

This particular stunt has worked well for a New York restaurant for many years, on an irregular basis. About every five years they roll back the prices to correspond to those of a turn-of-the-century landmark restaurant familiar to all New Yorkers. Each time it is done the event gets full media coverage—radio, television, and newspapers. Economists use it to explain the rate of inflation. Commentators use it to talk about the "good old days."

This is the kind of promotion in which long-term profits come from short-term costs, which is exactly what promotion is supposed to do for you—help your business by increasing your profits. Don't start a promotional stunt unless you've planned out all phases and you'll be able to carry it through. Simple as it looks on paper, there's lots of hard work and timing involved. If you have any serious questions as to its effectiveness, don't start. Long shots may be good for racing fans, but they're bad for the small business owner trying to build a growth pattern to success.

KEEPING IT SIMPLE

The tiniest promotional effort can become a twisted and complicated nightmare unless all factors are carefully considered in advance and planned for methodically. Overlook one vital piece of the puzzle and the whole effort goes down the drain, as the owner of a small department store learned.

The merchant decided to promote his toy business by giving free pony rides to his tiny customers—not an original idea, but one that seemed to him to be inexpensive and realistic. It turned out to be more complicated than he expected. First, a makeshift corral collapsed and another hitching post had to be brought in to replace the broken one, but the repairs were made in time for the event—so far so good.

A minimum of publicity had been done—a story in the local newspaper, some flyers sent to the elementary schools, and a small ad inviting children under six to take a free ride on Hansel or Gretel—the ponies. The promotion worked well, and crowds of eager children lined up for rides while their parents browsed inside—exactly what the owner had hoped would happen. The day was clear and sunny, and an extra policeman kept the traffic moving.

In such a perfect setting, what could possibly go wrong? All details had been covered—or had they? Just before the closing gong, one of the ponies nuzzled up to its expectant rider and took a small-sized bite, turning the successful day into a disaster. Newspaper and radio coverage produced the wrong kind of promotion for the store. A front-page picture told the world that "Gretel bites," going into the possible lawsuit and pinning blame on the store owner. Follow-up stories reported on the child's condition and terms of the out-of-court settlement—nothing a shop owner wants linked to his or her business.

So how can you protect yourself against such freak accidents? It turned out that a little careful checking could have prevented the accident. It wasn't the first time the pony had taken a nip from a customer—a fact that could have been discovered in advance. A hard and fast rule is that all live animals pose a potential risk in promotional events. In general, it's better to keep animals from direct contact with customers—especially children—unless it's Henny Penny with her teeth pulled and a muzzle over her beak.

The same goes for prizes which give away any type of live animals to children—turtles, rabbits, baby chicks, or stray kittens. Somebody is bound to complain if you give away trained fleas in a cage. The complaints are justified, since pets do pose problems, and small children are often thoughtlessly cruel to animals—it could be your luck to have your business forever associated with tortured turtles.

In keeping your promotional efforts simple, stick to the tried, the tested, and the uncomplicated. Save elaborate plans until you can afford to hire the proper help for their execution. And don't overcommit yourself in terms of effort, time, or money.

For example, unless you are a first-rate amateur artist, don't waste your valuable time attempting to draw clever figures in your promotional printed materials. And keep your writing simple, direct, and easy to understand, instead of fussing over literary style. It's not the literary quality of your words that will count, but the simplicity of your sales pitch that will drive home your message. Remember the controversy over the slogan "Winston tastes good like a cigarette should?" English teachers were up in arms because of the poor grammar, a fact which delighted the slogan's creator. The ad got extra attention, which sold more cigarettes, which was the purpose of the ad.

Measure your promotional campaign in these terms:

- What can it do for you?
- What can it do to you?
- How much will it cost?
- How much will it produce?

DON'T JUST SIT THERE—DO SOMETHING

So you've thought of all the pitfalls, weighed the pros and cons, checked out the competition, and surveyed the probable results. Don't sit there thinking while your profits slide out of sight in the wrong direction. Do something about it!

It is prudent to be cautious about promotion, but it is suicidal to do nothing. The quickest way out of business is to open shop and wait for the world to discover you. It is widely believed that if you build a better mousetrap, the world will beat a path to your door.

Don't believe it. You can build the best mousetrap in history, but unless you bait it with some good promotional ideas, the world will never know you have a path, a door, or a mousetrap.

FOUR

Publicity and the Media

*Publicity and Advertising / Advantages of Publicity /
Long-Range Publicity / Control—What You Can and Can't /
Contacts / Writing a Press Release / The Right Way and the
Wrong Way / Photographs / Radio and Television Publicity*

P UBLICITY CAN BE AS SIMPLE AS GETTING A ONE-LINE NO-
tice about a church meeting into a newspaper or an announcement of a tennis match on radio/television. Or it can
become as complicated as a Soviet five-year propaganda plan.
The trick for the small business person is to keep publicity
simple, direct, and effective. In order to do that, you'll need to
learn the rudiments of that vast number of publicity vehicles
loosely lumped together and called "the media," literally
translated as the medium. Media may sound as though it should
be singular, but it is plural—there are many media: newspapers,
magazines, television, radio, trade publications, shopping
sheets, and house organs. Any way in which you get your message to the public is your medium or media.

For the small business owner, that generally means newspapers, radio, and in rare instances television, if your community
has UHF or cable television. Since newspapers are the lifeblood
of small business—both for advertising and publicity—you'll
probably be dealing with newspapers more than with any other
single medium.

PUBLICITY AND ADVERTISING

The major differences between publicity and advertising are in
the cost and the control. Publicity is virtually free. Advertising is
not.

In advertising you pay your money and you get your space. You get as much space as you pay for—no more and no less. The space is yours to do with as you see fit, bounded only by the wide limits of the law. You can fill your space with words, pictures, or cartoons, or leave it blank. You are in total control.

Publicity reverses the control, because publicity is not for sale. (There are cases where it is sold under the table or tied to advertising but this is *never* ethical.) You cannot, for example, go to your local newspaper, buy space, and fill it with publicity which looks like news. If you try, your space will come out in print with a ring around it reading "advertisement, advertisement." A regular column has appeared for years in the *New York Times* with this kind of border surrounding it. Except for the border, the column looks and reads like any other column.

People have difficulty understanding the difference between publicity and advertising, because the overall objective for each is the same—both are designed specifically to sell or promote something. Publicity, just like advertising, is supposed to help your business. Whether it will do this or not depends upon the care and insight with which it is planned and executed.

Most publicity professionals have been confronted, at one time or another in their careers, by an irate boss or client who demands "front-page placement" for a press release. It continues to happen because the boss has little understanding of the business. Any professional who tries to comply with such unreasonable demands ends up with early ulcers, psychiatric treatment, or both. Publicity, at best, is a percentage, hit-and-miss business. It will never be an exact science. Results change from day to day because of many events impossible to control.

Since publicity cannot be bought, it must be created. Therefore it is the creativity that is bought. Buying the time of the people who create it has spawned a new industry of people dreaming up ways of getting publicity. Publicity has evolved into a support function for business—its objective to increase profits, the same as all other business functions.

In this evolution, the average individual seldom realizes that keeping events from happening has become as important in publicity as trying to make them happen. Many a corporate plan is derailed in the boardroom upon the advice of the communications vice-president, projecting unfavorable media reaction. The goal for corporate publicity can be to get favorable attention or, in certain cases, no attention at all. Business publicity is vastly different from celebrity-type publicity, although few people understand the difference.

ADVANTAGES OF PUBLICITY

The advantages of publicity for the small business are both obvious and subtle. It is obvious that free exposure is a godsend to many a strapped small business owner who can't afford a one-inch ad in a shopping sheet. Publicity may be the only way to reach a waiting public.

Less obvious are the long-range and continuous advantages publicity can bring you. Publicity, on the whole, is more believable than advertising. It is surrounded with the aura of truth and the implied endorsement of a third party—the newspaper. In publicity you are not perceived as trying to sell. In fact, your message must do more than sell, or it will probably end up in the trash barrel. Subtle publicity slides through the newspaper as news, while advertising is suspect. Indeed, if Solomon returned he would be hard pressed to separate the news from the publicity, so intertwined the two have become.

For example, suppose your business has set up a stunt in which a woman defies death by leaping off a tall building with an umbrella for a parachute. Is it news, publicity, or both? If the woman performs the stunt on her own, it is clearly news. But is the news value destroyed by your business name printed in huge orange letters on her parasol? Certainly not. Any fool who leaps from a building with only a parasol between life and death creates news. If the expected happens and she splatters like a bug on a windshield, it's news. And if she becomes the first person to parasol-glide to earth, it's bigger news. With or without your sponsorship, such an event is news. City editors by the dozens would end up in the booby hatch if they attempted to fine-sift news from publicity. It cannot be done. It isn't because editors don't know the difference—far from it. It is because they are involved in trying to make their businesses succeed, the same as you, and newspapers thrive on enthusiastic readers.

A newspaper which ignored all news tainted with publicity would go out of business. It would also be placed in the position of rejecting press releases from the White House. The President, through publicity, also puts his best foot forward. So should you.

LONG-RANGE PUBLICITY

Long-range publicity, planned with your business goals in mind, is sane, sound, sensible, and best of all, virtually free. You need not go about it so aggressively that you get the reputation of being a publicity hound. But understanding that publicity is helpful, legitimate, and appropriate can give you an edge over your competitors who continue to feel uncomfortable seeking publicity. It's only human to be leery about publicity at first, but as you understand its legitimate function in your business, you'll get to be an old hand at recognizing opportunities or creating them. You will instinctively gravitate toward productive publicity, not wasting valuable time on ego puffery which provides nothing except fillers for scrapbooks.

In recognizing effective publicity, pay close attention to what is known as "press relations," a foggy term with various implications—generally wrong. "Press relations" means nothing more than exercising good, common sense in dealing with professionals in the newspaper business. Naturally, you should treat people in the news business like everybody else—with courtesy, honesty, and consideration. And since you need them in order to make your publicity work, it's wise to get to know their turf.

The inside workings of newspapers are foreign territory to most people, many of whom have never set foot inside one. If you were planning a trip to a foreign land, you'd probably bone up on the people and their culture—at least enough to avoid making a sizable blunder, like ordering steak in India.

CONTROL—WHAT YOU CAN AND CAN'T

Where advertising puts you in the driver's seat, publicity makes you a passenger. Worse still, you're a free passenger. Any time the driver wishes, you can be tossed out of the bus. It is an uncomfortable position, especially for those persons who are used to being in control. If it's any comfort, the greatest pain is suffered by the biggest executives or politicians—those whose slightest command is instantly gratified by a horde of underlings. Quite regularly, a public relations staffer is sent out of the chairman-of-the-board's office with an explicit four-letter reply to a newspaper's inquiry. The publicity person routinely translates the message into less explicit language, knowing the quote may end up verbatim in most papers, and in suggestive dashes in the *New York Times.* It's not a prudent way to behave, but it's human.

So, accept the limitations of your passive role in placing publicity, and substitute creativity, persistence, and meticulous preparation for control. Learn early those things over which you have no control. They include:

- *Printing:* You think you have a world-shaking announcement, but it hits the newspaper wastebasket. If you and the editor disagree over the value of a story, there is no contest. You lose.
- *Placement:* You believe your press release or idea deserves front page. The editor thinks it fits fine in two lines at the bottom of the obituary page. You guessed it. You're on the obituary page.
- *Timing:* You have a story which *must* get into the paper immediately. Tomorrow is too late. The story is overset (print set aside for later use), and your urgent phone calls produce yawns at the newspaper. After a week, stop looking. The overset has been replaced with more overset.
- *Content:* You've worked two weeks on a first-class news release, and every word has been polished until it would shame Shakespeare. When it gets into print, it has been cut to ribbons and sliced into slivers. It now reads like Norman Mailer talks. Your complaints will be received like a condemned killer's protests to the jury after the verdict is read. Save your breath.
- *Omission:* Your perfect press release which followed good journalism rules comes out in print with the date omitted.

The newspaper has violated its own rule of "who, what, where, when, why and how" by leaving out "when." If your request to correct the omission is ignored, forget it. Buy an ad to fill in "when." You've had it.

- *Complaints:* Is it ever appropriate to complain to a newspaper, or must you live with the theory that the meek shall someday get a decent break?

    Complain only if it is really important, and be positive. If your releases have been hitting zero, go—in person—to the newspaper and ask why. Go after deadline. You'll generally discover you are the one causing the problem. Note any specific procedure the newspaper has for press releases and follow it exactly, no matter if they tell you to drop all releases down their chimney. Their rules are their rules. Keep in mind that in publicity nothing counts except the end product—getting into print.

CONTACTS

"Contacts"—another fuzzy word with vast implications. It implies that well-placed friends in the news business will make publicity easy for you and ballyhoo any widget you want to sell. Don't believe it. Nothing is further from the truth.

Friends on newspapers are like friends elsewhere. They'll talk to you, except on deadline, but they'll quickly tire of putting their jobs on the line for your publicity. If you pressure them for favored treatment you'll strain the friendship, just as they would if they expected your goods or services free on demand.

Friends can be helpful in giving you an inside look at their operations, plus an occasional favor if it is reasonable. But depending upon friends for regular publicity is like borrowing sugar from a neighbor. The third time you show up with your empty bowl, you're likely to be curtly handed a map to the nearest grocery.

Newspaper friends can be valuable, but their value is subtle and their judgment of publicity hounds impeccable. They can give you a slight edge by the following:

- When friends see your name at the top of a release, you'll get the benefit of the doubt—if there is a doubt. That means you'll get in the paper quicker than a stranger with an equally good story.

- When press people learn they can trust you and your judgment, you'll get better coverage than somebody they don't know about.
- Contacts will give you a break sometimes on a second-rate story, especially in an early edition that needs filling.
- Contacts may tell you, bluntly, whether publicity you are planning will work or bomb.
- Contacts can give you helpful information about the news business in general and about their newspaper specifically.

WRITING A PRESS RELEASE

Most people who aren't professional writers (and most who are) have trouble writing. A person who talks in short, clear, crisp sentences writes in unknown tongue. The crisp sentences are blurred with big, impressive words and gibberish phrases. Periods are used as sparingly as fifty-dollar bills. The finished product reads like a legal contract.

A famous journalism professor says that high school graduates are the world's worst writers because they are educated enough to understand big words, but not educated enough to realize that little words work better.

Use the fewest number of words in communicating any thought. (There are some well-known gestures that require no words, yet express volumes.) The purpose of writing is to transfer an idea from your head to the heads of others. Too many words—especially big words—muck up the meaning and leave room for misunderstanding. When you write "stop," it's hard to be misunderstood—but when you write "desist," it becomes easier. Never use a big word or a less common word if a commonly used little word conveys your meaning. Never use a complex sentence if you can use a simple sentence. Don't expect writing to be easy. It isn't. If it's easy for you to write, you can be sure it will be hard for the reader to read. Easy writing makes hard reading.

In writing a press release, begin by jotting down notes to yourself, answering some basic questions that your press release must cover. For example, suppose you are the owner of an appliance store and your business has sponsored a community bowling league for several years. You want to get a story in the local newspaper, announcing the new bowling season and tying in your sponsorship. Answer these questions:

- *Who?* Ace Appliance Store.
- *What?* Sponsorship of bowling league.
- *Where?* Local bowling alley.
- *When?* Monday, 7 P.M.
- *Why?* Community service/business/fun.
- *How?* Ace Appliance supplies uniforms, pays all costs, is hoping for a championship season, has a good chance.

You've sketched out the bare-bones facts of a press release, but unless you do some fancy footwork your press release will put everybody to sleep, beginning with the sports editor. Nothing you have listed will get you more than two lines on the sports page, and maybe not that.

Take a careful look and add interesting facts to your skeleton. What interests you will probably interest others, since the majority of people are interested in pretty much the same general things:

- You, the owner of the Ace Appliance Store, are a champion bowler.
- Your team came in second in the local tournament last year.
- There's more interest in bowling in your town than in any other sport.
- Your team is mixed, with both men and women playing, unlike most teams.
- Your wife is a member of the team that beat your team last year.
- You've retaliated by recruiting the wife of the opposing team's captain—which will be revealed, for the first time, Monday night.

Now you have something interesting going for you. You have several possible angles to lead off with: the contest between two rival teams; oneupmanship in recruitment; the suspense of your surprise announcement; or a combination of all. You can announce your new team member or keep it secret and try to interest the sports editor in covering the event, telling him or her in advance what the surprise is. If you decide on this approach, your press release could read something like the following:

Easy Ace Bowlers   [Date]
Contact: Joseph Ace
ACE APPLIANCE STORE, sponsor
110 Main St.
Fairway, N.D. 11330

551-8890
559-6789 (home)

FOR IMMEDIATE RELEASE

The Easy Ace Bowlers, runners-up in last year's tournament, promise to reveal a powerful secret weapon at the season's opening game, Monday at 7 P.M. at Fairway Lanes.

Sponsor Joseph Ace, owner of the Ace Appliance Store, 110 Main Street, Fairway, made the announcement.

"We've been steaming all summer over those points that cost us the tournament last fall," Ace said, "and we're hot to get it back this year. If we don't, I can't go home and face my wife."

Mrs. Ace is a team member of the Ridge Runners, last year's champions, which narrowly edged the Easy Aces last September.

"Joe talks big, but he doesn't scare us," Mrs. Ace said in commenting on the special announcement. "We don't care if he has recruited the Abominable Snowman—we'll beat them again."

The two teams will face each other in a special season opener. The game will begin promptly at 7 P.M. The public is welcome.

Timing Your Release

The Ace Appliance Store owner properly planned his press release about ten days in advance of the event, which gave him time to:

- Phone the sports editor and talk to him or her about the story.
- Suggest coverage of the event and discuss picture possibilities.

- Give the newspaper several days to fit in the press release, which increased its chances of being used.
- Be certain of press release delivery—in person or by mail.

The best possible results for the Ace Appliance Store owner would be an advance story about the event plus in-person coverage by the newspaper, a follow-up story complete with pictures. Should these fortunate circumstances occur, the following objectives would have been accomplished:

- Positive event tied to business—good for community, good for business.
- Increased awareness of the Ace Appliance Store.
- Positive image of businessman in community.

But did it sell appliances? Not directly, but indirectly. The following year Joe Ace was chairman of the Community Chest Drive and served on a committee to build a town swimming pool. His community thrived and his business prospered. Publicity was a piece of the puzzle of his business success.

Press-Release Pointers

If you are the proud owner of a press release which proves that Amelia Earhart is alive and well and living in a cave in Scotland, you can scrawl it on the back of a brown paper bag and get it printed. All rules are out. It's a hot story. But for those thousands of less grabbing press releases, the ones you want in the newspaper more than the editor wants them in, follow a few basic rules:

- Put date in upper righthand corner.
- Identify the contact; this makes it easy to reach you if release details need to be clarified.
- Put release date a few spaces from the contact identification; e.g., FOR IMMEDIATE RELEASE; FOR RELEASE AFTER FEB. 3RD.
- Headline optional; e.g., ACE BOWLERS REVEAL SECRET WEAPON.
- Type, double-spaced, on standard 8 1/2 × 11 paper.
- Begin a third of the page from the top.
- Use short sentences.

- Answer the questions raised by who, what, where, when, why, and how.
- Leave comfortable wide margins—never crowd.
- Identify story in upper lefthand corner of second page. Pages sometimes get separated at newspaper.
- Address the release to the specific department; e.g., Sports Editor—plus specific name of editor.
- Indicate the end of your release; use # #, * * * or -30-.
- If release needs explanation, make it a very short note.

Placing Your Press Release

"Placing" a press release means getting it to the right person, at the right time, in order to maximize your chances of getting the release printed. Direct, personal placement is best. Personal placement gives you the chance to explain the release briefly, and it eliminates a dozen ways the release can get lost if you don't deliver it in person.

When you show up at the newspaper's reception desk in person with your press release in hand, it is still superior to mail or messenger, even if you don't get in to see the editor or reporter involved. You can hand the release to a receptionist, give explicit instructions where and to whom it is to go immediately, and await confirmation that the release reached its proper destination. Yes, wait and ask, "Did you hand the release to so-and-so?" If the answer is, "I put it in a basket on so-and-so's desk," you have more work to do. Phone for confirmation later and make sure the release found its way out of the basket. Many releases have died there.

If you can't manage direct delivery, a messenger is next best, and if you can't manage a messenger, you can institute some supports for the U.S. mails. Never drop a press release in a mailbox and assume the best. At the most critical time, the worst will happen. And never mail a press release without keeping a copy. The possibilities for error are limitless: the release can be delivered to the wrong address; it can get delivered to the wrong department after it reaches the newspaper; it can be delayed in the mails; it can be permanently lost or end up in Paris two years hence. The easiest explanation of why it never got printed is that the release never reached its destination. Sometimes that's not true—it's just an easy explanation. Regardless, your hard work will be down the drain.

Find out how the newspaper is organized—its various departments—and save yourself time by getting your release to the proper department and person. Never call near a deadline to ask for any kind of information. Learn deadlines and respect them. Remember that a reporter may be jammed up at any time, day or night, so always ask before you have a leisurely chat. When you learn the newspaper's structure and personnel, keep records. List names, departments, deadlines, and note any changes. In most newspapers, the faces change frequently as people go on to new jobs. If you haven't kept your records up to date, you'll be starting from scratch. In many areas covered by clipping services, media listings are printed for outside distribution by the clipping service. Before you do the work yourself, find out if it has been done by the clipping service. The few dollars for the book will be well spent.

THE RIGHT WAY AND THE WRONG WAY

A newspaper reporter covering an event is greeted by the chairman, who says, "Oh, the *Village Sentinel.* I am a good friend of the editor. Tell George I'm keeping my eye on you, and spell my name right this time—huh, Mac?"

A woman marches into an afternoon newspaper office at 11 A.M. and demands to see the editor. "I want this editorial about our hospital fund drive in the paper Tuesday, a week from today," demands Mrs. Important.

A reporter calls a press release contact to check on a name in the release. "No, I'm not sure of the spelling," says the contact. "But look it up. It's in the book, you know."

The owner of a local department store calls the editor of a newspaper, "I want that release printed, or I'll pull out all my advertising," says Mr. Bigshot.

These are obvious ways of making enemies and influencing nobody, but there are other, subtler ways to do the same thing. Out of ignorance, people mangle personal and business relationships. In your dealings with all media people, try to understand the situation from their point of view. How would you feel placed in their chair? Bad manners make bad business. Here are a few do's and don'ts:

- *Don't* throw your weight around, not even if the publisher is your uncle.
- *Don't* ask a friend in another newspaper department to get a sports story in the paper.
- *Don't* play one newspaper off against another. Be fair with both.
- *Don't* go over a reporter's head or an editor's head, except for the most serious offense. Work the problem out directly with the person involved.
- *Don't* exaggerate the importance of a press release. Your store opening is not as newsworthy as the mayor's resignation.
- *Don't* leave information holes in your press release. Be sure of your facts and be sure they are all included.
- *Don't* complain if your release is rewritten, cut, or left out completely. Tomorrow brings another newspaper and another opportunity.
- *Don't* get angry, no matter how right you are. Be positive, persistent, and fair.
- *Don't* demand a retraction for unimportant details just because they were printed wrong.
- *Don't* send lavish gifts or try to buy your way into a newspaper.
- *Don't* lean on newspaper friends. If they can do you a favor they will. If not, don't discuss it.
- *Don't* threaten a newsperson unless you plan to lead an exemplary life in the future.

- *Do* be helpful. Do as much work as possible, so a reporter's job will be easier. Spell names correctly, make sure every fact is a fact, call up with tips about other stories, give background information about stories unrelated to you if you can.
- *Do* trust reporters. They will—almost always—honor your "off-record" comments *if* it has been made clear that what you are saying is off the record. Make sure!

- *Do* honor an exclusive story. A reporter will never forget the person who costs the paper an exclusive.
- *Do* be businesslike and avoid long conversations.
- *Do* give credit where it's due. Call up, or write a note of thanks, when a newspaper person has been helpful to you. Most people call newspapers to complain.
- *Do* take interest in the newspaper. Be a regular reader.
- *Do* understand that 50 percent, or more, of your releases will end up in the garbage. It is not a conspiracy. Nobody hates you or your business. It happens to all. A 50-percent placement rate is something to be pleased about—not dejected.
- *Do* tell a reporter if something is incorrect in the paper. It will probably be corrected next time.

PHOTOGRAPHS

If you have a sensational publicity idea with good picture possibilities, the newspaper will probably send its own photographer to cover the event. By all means suggest it. But if you get a turn-down, go on to the next possibility, which is supplying the newspaper with your own photographs. When it works it enhances your press release measurably.

Try to take interesting photographs instead of the run-of-the-mill poses everybody sees ten times a day: stiff wooden people; awkward positions; cluttered background; unexplained detail; the overused handshake; too dark or too light; the posed first spadeful of earth; key to the city; girls on cars; girls on bear rugs; girls on tigers; girls smiling blank smiles in beauty pageants. Think up a new angle and go slow on the cheesecake—it will make more enemies than friends.

The newspaper can use almost any photograph you give them except those so badly exposed they can't be printed. Sometimes a well-cropped photograph (cutting out certain details) comes out looking good when you didn't expect it.

Be sure that you write a cutline for the photograph—an identifying line or two at the bottom of the picture. Paste it onto the photograph (never clip) and fold back. Your cutline may say something like: "Three-pound tomato grown by Thomas P. Greenthumb, owner of Greenthumb Nursery, Main Street. Greenthumb's three-year-old daughter, Nancy, examines the tomato."

Make sure you protect the photograph by placing it in a cardboard envelope sandwich for mail delivery. A crumpled photograph won't be used.

Your own press release, accompanied by your own photograph, is a thing of joy for a small business person to see. The picture makes the story come alive as nothing else can. A photograph, although very important in publicity, is not worth a thousand press releases. But a thousand press releases will be more effective if accompanied by a thousand pictures.

RADIO AND TELEVISION PUBLICITY

A perfect press release for newspapers may never see air time on radio or television, because of the different requirements of the electronic media. Although the rules for good press relations apply to all alike, certain other rules are different. To get maximum results from your publicity, learn the special problems of each medium and fit your publicity accordingly.

Small radio and television stations welcome press releases. Like newspapers, they are in business to attract more listeners or viewers. If you create different, interesting, newsworthy publicity, you can be successful with radio and television. Human interest is human interest. But a newspaper press release mailed to a radio or television station doesn't consider special needs. Unless it tells your story in the first two sentences, it's likely to be discarded, and a shorter, punchier one substituted. Small stations are notoriously understaffed. There will be little or no assistance in rewriting your press releases unless they are recognized as exceedingly important news events—which is seldom the case.

You'll generally be dealing with radio stations, since every community has at least one station and many have more. Small television stations are still rare in most communities. The possibilities for using radio to your advantage in placing publicity are vast. You would recognize this immediately if you saw an empty radio log used to list each broadcast day's events. The log looks like the Sahara Desert; it takes a huge amount of material to fill one single day. In fact, if it weren't for music, half the radio stations would go quietly off the air.

The radio schedule is different from a newspaper's, inasmuch as every minute can be a deadline. A news bulletin can edge out the world's best press release as a fast-moving story is captured while it happens. Radio news ages faster than newspaper news. What seems usual in a newspaper seems dated in a radio newscast. The immediacy of radio can be an advantage for business, as was proved by a Community Chamber of Commerce in its annual Business Day Fair. On-the-spot coverage by the local radio station filled the grounds to overflowing by attracting motorists who were listening to their radios. No newspaper could have done this, since most of the motorists were Sunday drivers from a nearby city and didn't read the local newspaper.

Writing a Radio Press Release
It takes little extra time for you to write a separate publicity release for radio, especially if you have already written your newspaper release. All that's left for you to do is to cut down the size of the release without removing the important facts. All the vital material is before you.

Turn back to the Easy Ace Bowlers press release and allow yourself two paragraphs for a radio release. Your publicity objectives remain the same: getting your business on the air by providing an interesting event for the radio station which will appeal to their listeners. Put the same information at the top of your release as you did for the newspaper:

Easy Ace Bowlers   [Date]
Contact: Joseph Ace
ACE APPLIANCE STORE, sponsor
110 Main St.
Fairway, N.D. 11330

551-8890
559-6789 (home)

FOR IMMEDIATE RELEASE

The Easy Ace Bowlers, runners-up in last year's tournament, promise to reveal a powerful secret weapon at the season's opening game Monday at 7 P.M. at Fairway Lanes, according to Sponsor Joseph Ace, owner of the Ace Appliance Store, 110 Main Street.

The Easy Aces will face the championship Ridge Runners, the team that beat them last fall. Ace says he doesn't want to give the secret away, but it has something to do with *sex*. The public is welcome. Remember, game time is 7 P.M. at Fairway Lanes.

Your first paragraph is almost exactly the same as for your newspaper press release, but in your second paragraph you spiced up the story by throwing in *sex* and repeated the time and place of the game.

In placing the release, follow the exact same procedure as for placing newspaper publicity. Suggest that the station provide live or recorded coverage. Suggest interview ideas, and don't treat the radio station as an afterthought—second to newspapers. Get acquainted with the sports announcer—it may be the general manager, who wears several hats in many stations—and be as cooperative as possible. Go to the station in person at 6 A.M. if requested for a live interview. Also, when you can afford it, think of sponsoring a short program on radio—it's not as expensive as you think, and it has been successful for many a small business. (See later chapter on advertising.)

If there are any hard-to-pronounce names or words in your radio release, include the phonetic pronounciation. For example, the name Bernstein can be pronounced two ways. Write it like this: Burn'stein, rhymes with teen, or Burn'stein, rhymes with dine. Pronouncing strange names and places can be a nightmare for radio announcers, as can various word combinations and some words beginning with "s," which come out of a microphone in a whistle.

Radio publicity releases must "grab" quicker than a press release. You've a split second to interest the listener and keep his or her attention. Get a "hook" for your radio copy and get into your message fast. In getting the most mileage out of your release, send duplicate releases to any program or person at the station who might use it—not just to the central news desk. It's always better to waste a few stamps than to undercover the possibilities. The same as for newspapers, make sure your release has reached its proper destination and that all angles have been covered.

You'll find that small radio and television stations are responsive to suggestions. The radio station in a town like Fairway, which draws hundreds of bowlers to its most popular sport, will be anxious to provide coverage. After all, the station's business depends upon getting listeners. The more listeners the station attracts, the more their sponsored programs and paid spot announcements will be worth, and the more you—as a business owner—will want to advertise. Their needs and your needs meet to form a complete circle.

FIVE

Community Relations

THERE ONCE WAS A MAN WHO OWNED A SMALL BUSINESS BY the side of a busy road in a small midwestern town. He tended his store and paid no attention to what was going on around him in the little town. "I'm not a joiner," he would explain, each time he was asked to help out with activities in the community. "If people want what I sell, they will buy it. If people don't want what I sell, they won't buy it just because of the clubs I join, the dinners I go to, or the meetings I attend."

Good, sound, reasonable, down-to-earth thinking?

The next thing the small business owner knew, a road bypass turned his small business into one with more of a past than a future, while adjoining land was rezoned for an industrial neighbor he could easily have lived without.

Perhaps the state-mandated road would have gone through anyway, and the rezoning would have occurred if the businessman had been a member of every service club and business association, paid dues to both political parties, and cornered the market for the policeman's ball. But a lingering doubt remains in the back of his mind that his presence might have altered the outcome. At the very least, he would have been aware of the possibility ahead of the reality, instead of learning both simultaneously. Subtle and not-so-subtle influences make up every political decision. Minding the store no longer means what it did a century ago. Minding the store includes minding the community as well—labeled *community relations.*

But isn't it blatant opportunism to become a community do-gooder for the sake of business? Doesn't it make a business owner's every action suspect? It is a thin line which requires constant attention, because it is the line which separates good community relations from business opportunism. Everybody is familiar with the type of business owner who joins every organization in town and serves on every board or committee available, for the paramount purpose of pushing business and making profitable contacts. Every action is calculated to increase business profits.

But there is another type of business person—one who realizes that the success of business depends upon the stability and health of the community—that dedication to one demands dedication to the other. This kind of person will occasionally hand out ice cream cones to the softball team without sending out a press release. Such business leaders have also been known to take unpopular stands for the sake of their communities, when community needs and business needs collide. In the long run, good community relations will pay off instead of opportunism. There may appear to be exceptions, but opportunism isn't a recommended route.

"The most effective public service is often based on enlightened self-interest," according to Louis B. Lundborg, vice-president of the Bank of America, in his book *Public Relations in the Local Community.* "Nowhere is that more true than in the community field. Community relations undertaken solely for selfish purposes may backfire; but where the enlightenment is at least as great as the self-interest, both community and self may profit."

"But while there is no better business builder, in most lines, than active community contact," Mr. Lundborg continues, "it is a paradox that community activity will be a better sales builder if it isn't used for that purpose. . . . If you don't try to cash in, you will, and if you do try to cash in, you may fail entirely.''

YOU AND THE COMMUNITY

The mutuality of business and community is long-range. While big business can move its people around like chess pieces, the small business owner generally remains in the community for life. Therefore the community *is* his or her business. If the community prospers, the business prospers. If the schools attract new people, both the town and the business prosper. If the hospitals maintain good health, the health of the people maintained is the health of business.

The wise business leader has little alternative except to take an active role in the community, because of this interdependency. It is a realistic building block to business success—a mortgage on the future.

While paying your civic rent, however, it is important not to bite off more than you can chew, which frequently happens to business people who have difficulty saying no. Unless you are careful about making civic commitments, you may find yourself minding the community to the detriment of your business. Keep business and community on parallel lines. Your first objective in a tiny growing business must be business. Later, when you are more successful, you will have time to be a good samaritan.

Just remember, if you go broke nobody will talk about the uniforms you supplied the Little League or the Sundays you spent turning the town dump into the town park. People will shake their heads and wag their tongues about what a poor business manager you were—which will be true.

But remember that no matter how separate you attempt to be in a community, you—as a small business operator—are part of the community. You are surrounded by others doing business. Some buy from you and others sell to you. You are part of the political process—passive or assertive; part of various groups, the educational system, the religious community. All become intertwined in your business success as well as the success of the community. Your actions and reactions can work for you or against you.

THE BUSINESS COMMUNITY

A customer walks into a small gift shop and angrily demands to know why the shop owner cannot stock a particular item. "I asked you six weeks ago to order this for me," says the irate person.

"I know," says the shopkeeper sadly, "but I just can't seem to move the supplier—I don't understand the delays any better than you do."

This same shopkeeper reveals that suppliers are her main problem. "I finally threatened one with pulling out every one of his products—and he laughed in my face. He knows I need him more than he needs my business, since his products are well advertised nationally and there's a lot of demand for them."

Your suppliers—some of them business neighbors such as your banker—are indispensable to your success in business. It makes sense to treat your suppliers with the same kind of consideration you want from your customers (you are their supplier). Yet often business owners pay no attention to suppliers except with orders. Your relationship with suppliers may stay on an even keel for years, until a shortage occurs, or a strike, or anything to upset the delivery routine. Unless your supplier relations have been good, you're not going to be at the top of their service lists. Did you notice how some service stations were always out of gas during the gasoline shortage?—and not just the ones the big suppliers were trying to run out of business.

Aside from treating them decently because it is the decent thing to do, your suppliers know valuable information for your business. The supplier knows what's going on inside the business—new products, raw materials, new processes being developed. Don't neglect this storehouse of information which can be helpful to you. Put yourself in your suppliers' place and try to make their life a little easier. Do little things. Be friendly. Be interested. Be considerate. Someday, when all about you, others are not receiving orders, you will be receiving yours.

The same goes for other business people in your community, whether they are suppliers or not. Cooperate with the business community. All have common interests. You don't have to be enemies, not even with your closest competitors. Compete hard, but play fair. Don't steal help from other businesses. Recruit openly and honestly, and leave it to the employee to decide where to work. Secrecy in recruiting help, especially in small towns, has created a lot of bad blood among business owners. Many times the same offers, executed in the open, would have produced opposite results.

THE POLITICAL COMMUNITY

Back in the days of the hitching post and the general store, a small business proprietor's political community relations were fulfilled if he/she was on a first-name basis with the sheriff. Zoning wasn't even a germinating thought, parking meters were unheard of, and about the only restriction placed by the political structure on a business owner was to call the law before disposing of a dead body.

Those were the days of "free enterprise," but they are gone forever. Enterprise will never again be free of political pressures. The only issue confronting the business community of any town is "how much." The city fathers and mothers can ruin your business in one bold stroke by forbidding on-street parking if the nearest parking lot is a half-mile from your door. Those whose livelihoods are provided by other means constantly demand government intervention in business. Those in business reverse the argument and wonder why government meddles so much in business. If you're on the business side of this seesaw, you should know how important to your business the political powers of your community can be, and hence how important your community relations with the political forces.

Since the financial health of a community depends to a great extent on its business health, reality restricts politicians from too much business restriction, but many times what's good for one business can send another into bankruptcy. Sunday blue laws are good for some businesses and bad for others. Off-street parking is good for some and bad for others. Every time a law is passed, it hurts some and helps others.

For example, take the 55-mile-an-hour speed laws. Never has there been a greater demand for electronic devices to evade the law. Citizen's band radios are selling like hotcakes, and radar detectors are zooming to the top of the sales charts. At the same time, truckers are complaining that other business all over the country is being curtailed because of higher costs of slow deliveries.

The small business owner should join with other business leaders in the community to protect against unreasonable interference by government. In most towns the local Chamber of Commerce is active, but not so active that it can't always use more assistance from business owners. It is just as legitimate for business owners to group together for protection and pressure as it is for any group in the country. That most people believe political pressures from business produce lopsided results favoring business, says nothing good about business community relations. The alarming facts about the number of small businesses forced out of business disproves this in most places. It's up to you, as a business leader, to get your message to the politicians and the people.

COMMUNITY SERVICE

Service organizations, voluntary groups, civic clubs, are an important part of your community relations. Through such organizations you and your business can form valuable contacts and serve the dual purposes of community good and business health. The Rotarians, Kiwanis, Lions, and others are composed of a variety of community residents who make up your business customers. The Boy Scouts, the Girl Scouts, the Red Cross, the YWCAs, YMCAs, YM-YWHAs—dozens of groups offer opportunity for the small business owner to become an integral part of the community.

The religious community offers other avenues for service and contact with vast numbers of people, as well as the educational community. Many small business owners serve as school board members or as directors in religious activities. Others find various methods by which they can be helpful. For example, a local bank can offer a meetingplace for groups. Your business can display notices of school or church activities. You can provide a community bulletin board for clubs to display announcements. Any way you are helpful to a service organization will gain you recognition and friends. There are hundreds of less obvious tasks that add up to good community relations, aside from helping out in raising funds—the mainstay of business linkage to community groups.

Be inventive and creative in your approach to service organizations. When your business fits in with their community activities, join in and help make the activity a success while helping make your business a success. Sometimes a promotion is thought up by a local newspaper or radio station in which your business can participate. In one area, the local radio station sponsored a week's phone-in auction with merchandise donated by merchants and proceeds going to the Chamber of Commerce for community projects. Merchants in the area benefited in two ways: free advertising, when they donated services or products for auction, and publicity later in the use of the proceeds.

If your Chamber of Commerce gives the appearance of being permanently out to lunch, give it an idea transfusion which will be good for business and good for the community. Nothing perks up a community like alert, enterprising business leaders who practice good community relations by planning events with mutual benefits. The event can be anything from a business facelift to a flea market, a park clean-up to a hospital fund drive. Joining in with other business leaders can be fun as well as profitable.

YOUR BUSINESS IMAGE

A customer walks into a small store and hesitatingly offers a small package to the sales clerk behind the counter. "I'd like to return these light bulbs," he says.

"We don't take returns," says the clerk. "Can't you read, mister? It's written right here on the wall."

A customer walks into a small restaurant and sits down at a table. The table is covered with stains and there's enough food on the floor to feed a flock of homing pigeons. "Whatta you want?" says a pencil-poised waitress in a rumpled uniform two sizes too small.

"I want out of here," mutters the customer, heading for the door.

"Suit yourself, mister," the waitress yells after him. "It's no skin off my nose."

The owners of these establishments may be the crown princes of goodness or crown princesses of personality, but the customer has seen nothing behind the scenes—only the public image is showing.

Chances are you'll never hear a peep from the customer. Most people go away quietly and never return. And you'll certainly never hear about the problem from those causing your bad image. Yet this behavior comes from bad community relations—both with your employees and with the community. It will translate itself into lost profits.

There is a marketing concept keyed to profit through good community relations which says: Everybody from the floor sweeper to the business owner must think and act in terms of being part of the sales force.

Ideally, each sale you make should win for you a lifelong customer. There are businesses which have supplied the same families for generations. In fact, there is an organization in New York City called the "Century Society" for such businesses.

If the kid you hired to sweep up hit a customer on the backside with a broom, you'd fire him or her immediately. But inexperienced business managers put up with things just as devastating to sales: sullenness, bad manners, inappropriate dress, smart remarks, gum-chewing, indifference, hostility, dirty fingernails, and the old standby which drives customers up the wall, "It's not my department."

"I'll never shop at that market again," explodes a woman. "The clerk packed my eggs on the bottom of the bag and put dripping chicken on top of the cookies."

"Why don't you complain to the owner?"

"The owner knows about it. He's the one who hired the packer."

"What a lovely young woman," says another store's customer. "She went to the trouble of calling me up and telling me she has ordered the kind of picture frames that I've been trying to find."

Your customers, like all human beings, respond to personal attention. They like to feel special. If you make them feel special, they will keep coming back.

"Everytime I shop in a supermarket instead of my neighborhood grocery," said a woman, "I feel guilty. I feel like I'm being a traitor to a friend." This woman went on to explain how she feels like a stranger in the supermarket, but enjoys the friendly visit to her neighborhood grocery, plus the personal service the store provides. "What supermarket owner would go out in freezing sleet and help me start a stalled car?" she said.

In a small business you are part of your customers' lives. They discuss your public image with each other. They talk about the smallest details—unimportant to you, important to them: your interior decorating, displays, clean or dirty floors, rude or polite help, whether you say hello or not, the pat on the head you give their babies, how you dress, who you pal around with, how much you weigh, and what you had to drink last Saturday night.

Everything you do and say or authorize to be done in the name of your business builds your public image.

If you are recognized as a solid citizen, kind, generous, helpful, friendly—pillar of the community—it will help your business.

"The easiest way to make money is to learn what people want, and sell it to them," according to the Institute of Banking. "The fastest way to lose money is to offer something, regardless of what people want, and try to make them buy it."

Thousands of customers—that complex social mechanism known as the public, which seldom can agree on anything—do agree on one thing: They want business to be helpful. It makes no difference whether a customer is dealing with a multinational corporation or a hot dog vendor, the customer wants complete and total dedication to his or her needs. A cold hotdog on a stale bun won't do. If you put yourself in the shoes of your customers and respond to their needs, your public image will be secure and your community relations superb.

EMPLOYEE COMMUNITY RELATIONS

A small business owner seldom can afford a printed booklet explaining to employees company expectations, rules of conduct, and methods of serving customers, such as large companies are able to afford. But a few Xeroxed pages listing concise rules can save time, misunderstandings, and lost profits. In the long run, the time and money you spend will be well worth it. Don't expect employees to motivate themselves—it's a rare one who will.

According to a booklet published by the Small Business Administration entitled *Profitable Community Relations for Small Business*, motivation and training of employees is a place where many small business owners fall short:

The first responsibility of management in any community relations program is to motivate and train its people in the fulfillment of their duties toward building an image of a responsible and civic-minded firm in the mind of the community. Accordingly, the executive of a small business will be wise to ask the following questions:

1. Are my people properly trained for their respective jobs?
2. Do they really understand the intricacies of their positions?
3. Are they aware of the impression which they create through their contacts with people?
4. Do I, as manager, make a determined and conscientious effort to encourage my people in this aspect of their jobs?
5. Do I set a good example in my dealings with outside people?
6. Do I encourage my people to be active in the various community service and voluntary organizations of their own choosing?
7. Do I occasionally release them from work in order to attend special functions in performance of their duties for this type of organization?
8. Do I commend my people when they do something beyond the usual in creating goodwill for the organization?
9. Do I on occasion, for example, tell the telephone operator that she is doing a good job, or the salesperson, or the serviceman, or any other employee, when such is the case?

10. Do I occasionally sponsor "courtesy" campaigns within the company on behalf of and in support of those conducted outside by the local civic organizations?

Confidence in management has a very direct bearing on the subject at hand. Low employee morale leads to an unfavorable community standing. Management needs the confidence of its employees before it can launch a good community relations program. Only then can it permeate all its employees with the philosophy that the company is interested in good community relations. If the owner-operator of a small business sets the pattern by action and word, and lets it be known that he is vitally concerned about the future of the entire community, employees will follow suit.

Many times, the outside activities of employees (e.g., Boy Scout, church work, charity drives) can be fitted into the community relations program of their company. For this reason, management must know what community activities its employees are engaged in on their own initiative and what their attitudes will be toward any planned future activities of the company. Only then can management make the fullest use of its community relations assets.

The same booklet asks sixteen searching questions and provides a few tried and tested community relations techniques:

1. Do you have a policy that good community relations is a matter of top management courses?
2. Do you constantly guard against your business activities conflicting with public policy?
3. Do you recognize each of the groups which make up an important segment of your firm's public?
4. Do you take regular steps to see that each group receives the appreciation it deserves?
5. Do you maintain sympathetic and wholesome employee relations with even temporary help?
6. Do you have an established system for informing employees on what your firm stands for and how it functions?
7. Do you try to keep informed on what the public thinks of your firm?
8. Do you try to check what you hear and make improvements where needed?
9. Do you avoid high-pressure tactics in your community relations activities?

10. Do you make continuous and consistent efforts to improve your community relations skill instead of merely putting on sporadic drives?
11. Do you make a conscious effort to understand how government affects your business and to improve your relations with government agencies?
12. Do you insist that all your company's actions be completely honest and sincere?
13. Do you remind your employees constantly that selling, serving, and good community relations are inseparable?
14. Do you make it a point to consider what is best for the public at large as well as for your own private interest when major business decisions are being made?
15. Are your premises well kept and pleasing to the eye?
16. Do you have a policy of encouraging your employees to be active in community organizations of their choosing?

SIX

The Value of Advertising: A Case Study

A DVERTISING IS A SALES TOOL EVERY BUSINESS NEEDS— from the biggest to the smallest. There is no magic in producing effective advertising—just plain common sense. Any good business manager can learn to use advertising skillfully in order to maximize the possibilities of business success.

A business is like a jigsaw puzzle: management, personnel, finance, marketing, advertising. It functions smoothly when the pieces are in their proper places; each complements the other and fits comfortably into its niche, each pulls its own weight without strain by pulling together.

Advertising is most effective when the other parts of your business are humming. This is especially true of a small business, which conveys a sense of excitement in learning, growing, producing. Advertising is at its best in this kind of atmosphere. There is something to crow about, something to point to with pride, something to tell the world to come and get. Nothing kills the effects of advertising like a routine, worn-out, dried-out, tired business attitude which reflects itself in dull institutional-type advertising year after year. The same old Christmas ad, Easter, back-to-school, August sales—all that's different is the date.

Your advertising reveals whether your business is living in the past or looking to the future. Keep it alive, constantly looking for new angles to fit a changing world. When you use an old idea, get a new twist. By checking out a company's advertising, you can generally tell how well it is doing financially—and not by the size of the ad, either. There is a subtle, ever-present, overall message which reflects attitudes.

Running a small business is fun, even though it is hard work. It is interesting, challenging, and filled with opportunity. If the original excitement has gone out of your business, look back over your advertising for clues to when it happened.

"A stale business is much like a stale marriage," says a former small business owner who has grown into a large business owner. "If the spark's gone, seek some professional advice from a business counselor, an agency like the Small Business Administration, or business associates. But if all efforts to rekindle the flame fail, don't stay in business for the sake of the children's inheritance."

If you're in a rut, perhaps what you need to dig yourself out is increased profits—a big motivator. Effective advertising can increase your sales and reduce your selling costs. The secret to advertising is not how much you spend, but how effectively you spend it. In allocating advertising dollars wisely, you need to set goals and investigate all possibilities for reaching those goals via the shortest route. Advertising is a good focal point, because it forces you to consider each function in your business and how well it is operating. Advertising can never be a substitute for good management, no matter how big your budget. Rather, advertising requires the same tight, careful management as all other parts of your business.

Tomorrow, when you open the doors of your small business, imagine you are walking in for the very first time. Put yourself in the place of new customers. What's to keep them coming back? What can you do to improve your business instantly? Perhaps you can wash a grimy window and improve your shop's appearance, or you can remodel the entire store, your bookkeeping procedures, or your employee training, or get a new package for your product. There are thousands of improvement possibilities for every small business (and large ones as well).

Think positively, like the owner of a small camera shop on the West Coast. Ted's shop was in a small resort town, with such a stabilized business volume it was driving him to despair. He could predict, within a few dollars, his monthly and annual profit. Each morning he awoke with a small gray cloud over his shoulder, and he dreaded going to work. Neither was he wild about staying home. He knew exactly what each day would bring, right down to the tuna sandwich for lunch at the diner down the street. He had been in business for ten years and the routine was getting him down. Ted began to entertain thoughts of homesteading in Alaska, getting a small farm in the valley, raising chickens, panning for gold. All his fantasies had a common thread: They placed Ted in a position of responsibility only for himself—no customers, no personnel problems, no hassles with suppliers.

Finally his wife made a suggestion. She said she moved furniture when she became depressed, and even that small act sometimes gave her a fresh outlook. Ted, thinking it was a silly suggestion, merely smiled and remarked that now he understood why the furniture was moved so often. But the thought stuck in his head that day at work. By the end of the day he decided to try it on a larger scale. What the heck did he have to lose? he thought. He was slowly going batty.

He closed the shop for two weeks for a complete facelift—a new working environment, from the dirty, dusty display window to the cracked paint on the bathroom wall. His wife was surprised when he asked her to help, because Ted had insisted on keeping his wife out of his business except in extreme emergencies. His two full-time employees also volunteered to pitch in, they were so delighted with the prospect of getting brighter working surroundings. The four scrubbed and painted, laid new floor tile, and hung bright potted plants. Ted put in new soft nonglare display lights, both in the ceiling and in display cases. He figured out a more efficient traffic pattern for customers, papered one wall in metallic wallpaper, which added an appearance of depth, and removed the tattered shade on his small office window so he could see into his storeroom at all times—this too added depth. While he was doing the physical labor, he considered lines of merchandise he wanted to get rid of and new ones he wanted to bring in. He thought up ways of advertising his new start—a brand new opening, a contest giving away a home movie camera, using a distributor's film display to show the camera in use. As the work progressed, Ted took color photographs showing the dusty old shop and a final one showing the bright new shop. He kept careful cost records of the remodeling, because he decided that he wanted to get back the cost in one month. Impossible? Not at all. He did it and more.

The best thing that happened to Ted was that he got a new mental beginning—a fresh start in his head, which brought back the excitement he had felt when he opened his business. He became interested in better management and decided to take some evening courses offered at a local college. He found that managing a small business can be a never-ending source of excitement—a fascinating career. And he also did what experts advise malcontents who dream of homesteading in Alaska: He stayed with the business he knew best and changed what was possible to change—himself. He didn't follow a dream which almost always turns into a nightmare.

Ted also got a new partner in business—his wife, who was fighting the same "routine" desperation at home and needed a challenge of her own. Together they turned a dull business into an exciting one, moving to a new location the following year and keeping the old shop as a second store. Finally, they made enough extra profit to comfortably take a trip to Alaska, where Ted met a homesteader. By that time, it was as close as he wanted to get to becoming one.

You can do it too. Change the way you are looking at your business. Be critical. Begin with your advertising, and use it to examine all the pieces of your business success. It will work for you if *you* will work for you. Begin by taking the following test, suggested by the Small Business Administration.

SUGGESTED INCUBATOR ASSIGNMENT

Advertising is important to the successful operation of a small business. A lot of times, failures in a small firm can be traced back to poor use of advertising potential. The following questions point up areas that an owner or manager should be particularly concerned with. Do you know the answers?

---

*Lie Detector Test**

True or False

1. T F A large ad run once every two months will generally get better results than a series of small ads run every week.

2. T F The amount of money a retail firm should spend for advertising is determined largely by past years' sales.

3. T F For the most part, retail stores do not attempt to create a demand for the goods they carry.

4. T F If your store is organized on a departmental basis, the percentages of advertising spent in each department should closely conform to the average for the store.

5. T F The advertisement itself, rather than its position in a newspaper, determines the number of people that will read it.

6. T F Package inserts are a cheap and effective method of advertising for a store.

7. T F The best time for a small hardware store to promote and advertise camping equipment is in November, when clearance sales can be promoted.

8. T F Direct mail advertising is limited chiefly to large stores, because of the high cost in relation to additional sales.

9. T F Direct mail advertising is an effective method for introducing new products.

10. T F Radio advertising requires a different viewpoint from newspaper advertising.

11. T F A retailer, advertising a new line of style merchandise, would find the appeal to a customer's desire to possess things the best buying motive.

---

* From *How To Organize and Operate a Small Business,* California State Department of Education (instructional outline).

12.	T	F	Advertising will affect the sale of style merchandise more than it will simple merchandise.
13.	T	F	The merchandise manager is in charge of advertising in the large department store.
14.	T	F	Increased sales will not always justify the cost of advertising.
15.	T	F	Advertising will not sell a line of outmoded bedroom furniture that customers do not want.

SEVEN

Planning a Budget and Setting Advertising Priorities

Choosing a Budgeting Method / Setting Goals / Putting Your Budget on Paper / Revising Your Budget / Defining Advertising Priorities / Think Big—Sell Small / Be a Giant-Killer / Timing / Keeping Advertising Current

I N MOST SMALL BUSINESSES IT IS THE OWNER-MANAGER WHO plans the budget for all operating expenses, including advertising. You as owner know better than anybody else what you can and can't afford. No book, no individual, can tell you specifically where to advertise, what to advertise, when to advertise, and how much to spend on advertising. These are your executive decisions, and your business will rise or fall on your decisions.

CHOOSING A BUDGETING METHOD

Guidelines, however, are helpful in acquainting you with alternate approaches. So seek as much expert advice as you can in planning and laying out your budget, but keep in mind that generalized advice must be cut to fit your particular situation. Cut and fit and revise your finished budget often—generally upward. Few small business owners spend enough initially for advertising. Most cut corners, which is harmful to the growth of their businesses.

Sometimes it takes a deep breath and what seems like a wild gamble to scrounge up enough courage to budget properly for advertising. You've heard the old saying a thousand times, so keep repeating it as you plan your budget: "In order to make money, you have to spend money." Your first question, quite naturally, is: How much? How much should I spend, based on which formula? A percentage of profits? A wild guess into the future? The sugarbowl approach of borrowing one month from Peter and the next from Paul? There are many methods—some good and some bad.

Spending Whatever You Can Afford

At first glance this may seem sensible for a small business. After all, it makes more sense than spending what you can't afford. As usual, the decision isn't as simple as it might seem.

Spending whatever you can afford—as many small businesses do—is an approach which balances this month's receipts with next month's advertising. Small business owners do it because they believe that a stable budget will emerge from a few months of this hit-and-miss system. They believe that after, say, about a year, a look over the advertising ledger will point the way to a firm budget.

This system leaves you a sitting duck for impulse advertising when you've had a good month and leaves you inflexible when you haven't. You need to be free to increase or decrease your budget for sound business reasons. Many times you'll want to increase your advertising when you've had a bad month and decrease it when you've had a good one. Or you may increase on both counts, or decrease on both.

Spending whatever you can afford leaves out the most important ingredient for a small business—flexible long-range planning which allows you to tailor your budget to your particular circumstances. If you've been spending whatever you can afford for advertising on a month-to-month basis, find a better way. It is a luxury no small business can afford.

Keeping Up with the Competition

Spending whatever it takes to stay even with the competition keeps you in a constant reactive position just at the time you need to establish an active direction. Good business management demands assertiveness. Taking your advertising lead from your competitors says you respect their judgment more than your own judgment. It says you are a follower, not a leader.

Keep a watchful eye on your competitors, but have more faith in your own advertising judgment. Study your competitors' advertising, figure out their approaches, and learn as much as you can about their results. But never follow their lead. Part of a good advertising strategy is keeping two steps ahead of the competition. Even if you "borrow" a successful idea from one of your competitors, improve it, build upon it, and improve its results. As with almost everything else, there's seldom a really new idea in advertising—just variations on old themes. When you "borrow" from your competitors, you are borrowing what they have borrowed from somebody else.

So if you've been in a defensive advertising position, waiting to see what your competitors do and matching them week for week, special for special, try a new approach. You set the pace and let them follow you. After you're out front, never follow a pat formula for advertising. A set pattern is too easy for your competitors to figure out. Toss in a few surprises. Be creative in your approach. Why help your competitors, when you have all you can manage keeping your own head above water?

Percentage of Gross Sales

Allocating a percentage of sales is a popular way of figuring out an advertising budget. It's a set formula, easy to work with and effortless to figure out. It is used by many businesses, allocating anywhere from one to three percent of gross sales to plow back into advertising. It involves less bookkeeping than other methods, and it works well for many.

Like other approaches, however, this system leaves little room for mistakes or maneuvering. Spending a percentage of sales can lock you into a no-growth pattern, since you are basing your next business on your last business and, by necessity, looking backward instead of forward. Sometimes a boom period can give you room to try out new advertising approaches. And many times the best answer to a slump season is more advertising. A set gross sales allocation won't allow you to react to reality. Even though it seems fiscally trouble-free and can let you off the hook from worrying about your advertising budget, this system is as inflexible as spending whatever you can afford. It just looks a little neater on the ledger.

+ promote seasonally

Cost and Objective

A specific cost-and-objective system leaves you room to maneuver on many fronts. The bad part is that it is more complicated than other approaches, which means more valuable time to set it up and see that it works. "Cost and objective" means setting aside a total dollar amount for advertising, then breaking the total down into smaller amounts for specific objectives.

For example, instead of listing your advertising as "to increase sales," cost-and-objective accounting requires that you define clearly what kinds of advertising you will attempt in order to reach the objective. Instead of listing a generalized goal, you may list several parts of the general goal. Perhaps you want to reach new customers. What new customers? Where will you look? What will your appeal be? How will you reach them? What are your expected results?

The cost-and-objective approach forces you to figure out all the angles before you allocate the funds—not after it's too late to revise a bad guess. Will you advertise products or services? Specifically, which ones? Why? How? It allows you to see various parts of your business broken down into advertising appeal and profitability as tracked by your advertising dollar.

Per Unit Assignment

This method establishes an expense total for each product or service. Like others, it begins with your judgment of what you can afford to spend for each unit. It too is intricate, causing more record-keeping and dollar-tracking. Like the cost-and-objective method, the per-unit-assignment method provides a beginning for budgeting rather than a detailed program which is harder to revise.

Whether this approach will work for you depends on what business you're in and how many products you handle. If you run a grocery, the bookkeeping could take up all your time, but if you sell a basic product or offer a service with a single function, the unit assignment may work well for you. The results can be measured practically for maximum accuracy. At a glance, you'll be able to see exactly where each advertising dollar went and what it bought.

Advertising as an Investment in the Future

Although this approach looks to the future, it is risky, since it considers advertising as an investment, allocating a set amount based upon a growth guess.

Naturally, you expect advertising to be an investment in a new business, but such thinking can be carried too far. Advertising, like other parts of your business, should produce measurable profits. It should be accountable—a full-fledged member of the profit team. You wouldn't carry an unprofitable product line in your business indefinitely, would you? Unless your advertising produces measured results, get rid of the type of advertising you are doing and replace it with something that works. Each part of your business is an investment in the future. Treat the separate parts as equals and demand profit accountability from each.

SETTING GOALS

Whatever method of budgeting you finally choose, determine your problems, your objectives, and your expectations. Your budget is your roadmap to success. Study your budget and your business constantly, fitting, changing, planning. Profit builds through a series of short cuts in a treacherous journey. If you were planning a trip through shark-infested waters, you'd want your charts to be the very best guide. That's what your budget is to your business. Don't let it gather dust in a drawer.

PUTTING YOUR BUDGET ON PAPER

Now that you've decided how much to spend, the next step is putting the numbers down on paper. Consider it a money history, not hidden treasure. It matters little what kind of ledger or notebook you use, as long as you're happy with your system and your system works for you. Accounting ledgers in stationery stores are practical, but a loose-leaf notebook with ledger paper has the advantage of flexibility in removing or adding pages. Whatever you choose, put the months of the year across the top of the page or pages, along with your total advertising budget. List the separate advertising media you intend to use on the lefthand side of the page—newspapers, radio, direct mail, flyers, television, etc.

If you use a cost-and-objective or per-unit-assignment budget, you'll need supporting sheets for each advertising objective. The master sheet will show you how much you budget for advertising, and the supporting sheet will show the media, the size of the ad, the time the ad ran, and the measured results. The initial setting up takes up the most time. Write everything in pencil—a sharp pencil—since ink can't be erased. Pencil in the estimated budget for each month with the estimated monthly spread—uneven distribution to take advantage of the seasonal peaks and valleys.

Clip notes, or add pages, which will enable you to see at a glance which advertising produced what results months or years after it occurred. Never depend upon your memory for anything. Everybody thinks they will remember clearly, and nobody ever does. Unless you have total recall, join the throngs whose memory is a never-ending hourglass—details drop hour after hour.

REVISING YOUR BUDGET

When you have prepared your advertising budget and combined it with a system of measurement, revising your budget becomes crucial—the final piece of the puzzle. You're not flying blind. You know where you want to go. In revising your budget, constantly look for a better route to profitability. When you get positive results from specific advertising, you'll want to look over your budget to allocate more money for this type of advertising. You may add more money to your total budget, or you may move the figures of your budget around like chess players.

Jack operated a small cash-and-carry grocery in a suburban area where he drew customers from five surrounding small towns. For several months after his grand opening, he concentrated on newspaper advertising. Advertising in five papers—even juggling them around week after week—was getting too expensive. He just couldn't afford that much—but he couldn't afford to stop advertising. To add to the dilemma, he didn't know which newspaper to cut out, since he drew customers from all five towns.

Jack decided to try direct mail, combining it with irregular advertising in the five newspapers. He discovered he could cut his advertising budget in half by using this method. He also found that he was able to reach his customers and blanket his market area successfully.

First Jack revised his budget to cut down on newspaper advertising and include direct mail. Later he revised the budget again, to cut out all newspaper advertising. After that, he decided that his decision to cut out all newspaper advertising was too drastic, so he revised the budget again to combine direct mail with smaller newspaper ads, rotating these weekly in the five newspapers.

Every business owner must chart his or her own course by trial and error. Conditions change constantly. What works well one year doesn't work so well the next. So keep a sharp eye out for opportunities and revise your budget to match. Business is never so good that it can't get better.

DEFINING ADVERTISING PRIORITIES

Your first business priority is to scrape through this month to keep alive the possibility of scraping through next month. Survival. It's the real problem for thousands of small businesses.

But after survival come more complicated decisions:

- What should I advertise—goods or services or both?
- Should my advertising always feature some kind of price cut come-on?
- Should I emphasize myself, my employees, my business, all or part?
- If I advertise price-cutting, will quality be questioned?
- If I advertise service, will price be questioned?

Naturally, the answers will depend to a large extent on your knowledge of your area, your business, and the demands of your customers or potential customers. Regardless of the problems, think of your business in these terms:

- In what ways is your business different, outstanding?
- What do you offer that the competition can't duplicate?
- In what kind of marketing area are you located?

These are the starting points for your advertising decisions. To stay in business, you must take them all into consideration. To grow, you must combine them, advertise them, and strike the right note of appeal. Examine your marketing area, bearing in mind these facts listed by the Small Business Administration:

- The average independent store draws customers from not more than a quarter of a mile.
- The average chain store draws customers from not more than three-quarters of a mile.
- The average shopping center draws customers from as far away as 4 miles.

Can you buck the trend and draw from 15 miles? Some small businesses draw from more than 100 miles, but very few. The odds are against you, and it's risky to take chances with business odds until you are in a stronger financial position.

When you advertise outside your logical marketing area, you waste coverage. Narrow it down further, by getting answers to these questions:

- Who are your customers or potential customers?
- What income groups do they generally represent?
- What is their reason for buying? Price or quality? Word of mouth or advertising? Both? What quantities do they require?
- Where do they live? Near your business? At a greater distance than the national average?
- What appeal do you have for them? Your facilities, products, services? Which of those you offer is most in demand?

For example, there is a small fish market in Greenwich, Conn., which would not survive in many other cities. This market is dedicated to providing the freshest fish at what might be the world's highest price. In an area such as Greenwich—which is to corporation executives what Beverly Hills is to movie stars—the price of the product is less important than the quality. Customers in this area will pay twice the going rate for quality. The market flies fish from all parts of the country, ready for sale hours after they were swimming in trout streams or ocean currents. The exclusive customers don't complain about the price— but let the quality slip, and screams echo throughout the town.

This market could not survive in most areas of the country. The same success story is true for others in reverse. A small variety store in a low-income section of a big city thrives by selling cheap clothing and plastic articles that nobody in Greenwich would cart home for free. It sells cheap merchandise at low prices to people in the area who cannot afford better. This store wouldn't survive a week in Greenwich, nor would the fish store last two days in this low-income area.

Size up your marketing area and define your advertising objectives. The better you know your prospective customers, their wants, needs, and shopping habits, the more likely you'll be to pinpoint your advertising in the right direction. No matter what you've heard to the contrary, nobody can sell refrigerators to Eskimos still living in igloos. Don't hasten your old age by trying.

According to the Small Business Administration, the consumer buying cycle begins with advertising and ends with a purchase through advertising appeal.

THE CONSUMER BUYING CYCLE*

Long before they visit a store, most customers do preliminary shopping in their homes through newspaper and magazine advertising, television and radio commercials, and direct mail literature or circulars delivered to the home.

When customers do go to a store, it is only natural that they go to the ones whose names, products, and services are familiar to them through advertising. In making purchases, customers almost always go through the following steps:

1. They are made aware of the product and service through advertising.

---

* From U. S. Small Business Administration, *Administrative Management Course Program,* 1976.

2. They are stimulated to know more about it by the advertising appeal.
3. They go to a store to investigate.
4. They analyze benefits and compare value.
5. They then make a decision, helped by point-of-sale promotion and intelligent selling.
6. They are satisfied and buy.

You can see that advertising is one of your most important budget items, because it attracts to your place of business the shoppers and customers who make it possible for you to meet your expenses and make a profit.

ADVERTISING APPEALS

To understand the job your advertising will have to do, you must look beyond material features or the obvious and search out the intangible appeals that cause people to buy. People don't buy things—they buy goods that satisfy their wants. Every product or service that is marketable has some benefit that the potential customer must see and want before you can ring up a sale.

People Buy Want-Satisfaction

A toothpaste maker uses these appeals:

It helps to remove dingy film.
It penetrates crevices.
It washes away food particles.
It cleans and beautifies the teeth.

A motor-oil refiner uses these:

It gives a motor pep and power.
It provides a quicker get-away.
It dissolves sludge, carbon, and motor varnish.
It saves up to 15 percent in gas and oil.
It frees sticky valves and rings.

Things People Want

People's wants are fairly standard. Most will react to one or another of the following appeals:

Convenience or comfort.
Love or friendship.

Desire for security.
Social approval or status.
Life, health, and well-being.
Profit, savings, or economy.
Stylishness.

THINK BIG—SELL SMALL

In selling "smallness," here are a few possibilities to include in your advertising which will give you a competitive advantage over big business:

- Personal service.
- Quality.
- Fast service.
- Responsive service.
- Time-saving products/services.
- Uniqueness.
- More effective guarantees.
- Ease in returning merchandise.
- Mutual interests and concerns.
- Special payment arrangements.
- Personal desire to serve needs.
- Ability to serve needs.
- Friendship.
- Stability in community.

Many small businesses cleverly exploit the frustrations customers feel in dealing with big business. Like the small dress shop, competing with larger department stores, whose monthly statements end with the note, "If your bill is incorrect, please phone us. A real human being will answer."

BE A GIANT-KILLER

Although you, along with most small business owners, feel insignificant in comparison to the country's giants, there are advantages to little business that cannot be matched by big business. Smallness, in itself, can be an advantage.

No matter how many books and movies project a robotlike existence for human beings in the future, people continue to behave quite similarly to human beings of earliest recorded history. Basic human needs don't change. Different ways of supplying those needs are what change. And many of those "mass" supply routes have broken down because they just haven't worked.

There's not a person alive today whose life remains untouched by mass production—big suppliers for small needs, who can turn a head gray overnight. Too many cogs in those big wheels fail to operate the smooth way the Madison Avenue copywriter writes it. A few well-managed corporations do respond instantly to customers, but most react like a dinosaur at top speed—about two miles per hour. "I keep wondering," says an irritated skeptic whose car was recalled by General Motors, "who's in charge of the quality control of quality control?"

Every time big business makes another enemy, small business has the opportunity of gaining a friend, and an advertising advantage. If you notice carefully, Madison Avenue constantly cuts the giants down to size in advertising, appeals to the consumer on the basis of smallness—a one-to-one approach. While they must twist and turn the truth in order to do this, the real thing can work for you. You are small. You do care. You are close to the consumer. You can be found when a product bombs. Your phone number is in the book, and the consumer can call the president of your company—you. In fact, they might get the president on the first ring. So, choose your advertising priorities to spotlight your advantage over big business. That way you can take on a Goliath and, like David, win with a slingshot.

TIMING

Timing is probably the most important single element in planning effective advertising priorities for most small businesses. Business—in almost every field—fluctuates from month to month, year to year, and season to season. Timing your advertising priorities to the pattern of your area means taking advantage of special events, or creating your own special events to fit in with the community. If you own a business in a college town, plan your special advertising around the college program: football season, orientation, early Christmas specials for your temporary customers.

Each community has its own pattern. A local nursery should keep in touch with the local gardening club; a bookstore with the local library; a sports shop with sports activities. It's important to know your town well, as most business owners do, but there are always those who are out to change the world instead of selling to it. For example, an East Coast builder several years back decided to go all-out in building Cape Cod and Swiss Chalet homes in an area of low-to-the-ground, Spanish-style housing. The builder figured it was time for a change, but his potential customers didn't. The only thing that changed was the builder's bank account.

As a general rule, people don't want their lives disturbed with too much change. Change tends to be slow and gradual—the kind that creeps up without disturbing the peace. Business is tagged with a conservative label since, by its nature, it supplies people's needs instead of creating them. Making business friends is not the same as making personal friends, although they may become synonymous at times. A profit-and-loss sheet promotes a simple philosophy: "When in Rome, do as the Romans do unless you discover something that sells better."

KEEPING ADVERTISING CURRENT

The Small Business Administration, as well as many businesses, needs to catch up to the economic reality of selling to women. As the SBA points out, women exercise purchasing power. But that purchasing power is not what it used to be—primarily as homemakers who bought goods and services for their families. Instead, women are going to work outside the home at the rate of a million a year and currently make up 40 percent of the country's work force.

According to the Department of Labor, the stereotype of the wife-homemaker, husband-breadwinner is valid for only 34 out of 100 husband-wife families today, compared with 56 out of 100 a quarter of a century ago. The shift is producing enormous economic change, slowly being recognized by the business community. As the two-income family increases, the buying habits of Americans change. Men push grocery carts and women buy automobiles. It is no longer safe for any business owner to direct advertising to males or females on the strength of traditional assumptions about male and female roles. In fact, a business continuing traditional advertising may alienate potential customers.

In choosing your advertising priorities, keep current with society's trends. Read widely enough to understand what is going on in your town and the nation as a whole. You don't have to personally agree with a particular trend in order to recognize a business opportunity it may offer. Your objective is to sell as much to as many people as possible, within the bounds of business ethics.

For example, a new housecleaning service took full advantage of the rising employment trend for women while an insurance company stumbled and fumbled. The cleaning service advertised "a total service—a new concept for the working family." The ad pointed out that while nobody can take the place of a mother or father, a cleaning service can replace them in such ways as cleaning an oven or waxing a floor. The ad concluded with a catchy line: "Put your spare time where it counts—with your family—and leave the cleaning to us."

In contrast, the insurance company advertised its ignorance along with its wares. A bold headline over the picture of a man proclaimed: "Some straight talk to the head of the house." The ad went on to discuss insurance as though only men bought insurance. The company committed the following avoidable advertising sins:

- Missed potential buyers by narrowing appeal to men only.
- Made unnecessary enemies of employed women.
- Exposed the company's ignorance about the number of female heads of households, not to mention those households operating on the theory of co-equals.
- Gave the company a horse-and-buggy image.

No matter if the insurance company's president secretly supports chaining women to the kitchen stove, it was bad business for his company to limit sales possibilities. Obviously, the company didn't want to make enemies. It was merely continuing to advertise the way it had advertised for years, ignoring the changes in society. Ten years ago the ad would have been acceptable. Today it isn't.

The cleaning service avoided falling into another trap by:

- Appealing to the family, not just the wife.
- Keeping all women happy in recognizing the value of a father as well as a mother.
- Gaining total agreement in recognizing that child care is more important than housecleaning.

Had this ad proclaimed in bold headlines—as many have—"Attention: Working Women," it would have created another kind of hostility, seldom recognized. Stay-at-home wives also consider themselves "working women," regardless of what the world considers them.

EIGHT

Selecting Your
Advertising Media

*Newspaper Advertising / Rates and Coverage / Specialty
Publications / Radio Advertising / Television Advertising /
The Yellow Pages / Gimmick Advertising / The Silver
Screen / Billboard Advertising / Local Transportation /
High School and College Publications*

YOU'VE STRUGGLED THROUGH PUTTING YOUR BUDGET down on paper and planning your advertising priorities. Now you have to decide where to put your hard work—which media to bet on, which combination to go with. How do you maximize your precious advertising dollars? If you advertise in several places, will it stretch your budget too thin? If you don't, will your message be spread too thin? How will you pick and choose and come up with the media which reach the right audience—your marketing area? These are critical decisions. The health and future of your business depends upon your answers. Assuming your business sells a necessary service or product, advertising is the final link in the success chain.

NEWSPAPER ADVERTISING

Newspapers, naturally, come to your mind first. That's because a lion's share of the small business advertising dollar goes into newspapers. Daily and weekly newspapers are the primary advertising medium of small business, and for good reasons. They effectively reach more consumers than any other media. For many small businesses, newspaper advertising is the only kind they do.

A newspaper's circulation can be multiplied by three—good news to you—since each copy is generally read by several people.

A family is counted as one subscriber, in circulation figures, even though it may be a family of two parents and ten children—all newspaper readers. Therefore, there's a good reason why newspaper advertising is the mainstay of small business: It produces results. Surveys have shown conclusively that readers read the advertising as much as the news content of newspapers. Long before a customer shows up at your door, he or she has done extensive newspaper shopping. Why, after such extensive shopping, an individual chooses your specific door is a fascinating question for the small business owner. In its answer lies the key to your success.

RATES AND COVERAGE

Since advertising rates are based on circulation, you need to look closely at the figures. A small local newspaper with far less circulation may be a better bet for your business than a regional newspaper reaching thousands beyond your market area. What you need to find, ideally, is a newspaper that matches—exactly—your market area. Since you'll probably have to settle for something less, shop around and match your area with a newspaper's subscribers. And keep in mind that the average business draws from a relatively small radius. It will be a helpful tidbit to throw out when an ad salesperson from a metropolitan newspaper knocks on your door.

However, a number of large newspapers with vast circulations are beginning to compete for advertising through special sections or pages devoted to specific locations—and advertising rates match the lowered circulation. So before you turn away a metropolitan paper's ad salesperson, check out their special selections, competitive rates, and circulation in your area.

In selecting a newspaper, first find out the number of newspapers in your area. You probably think you know—but unless you live in a very small town, you probably don't know. For example, Jan was planning to open a small antique shop in a community near a large city on the East Coast. To her amazement, she discovered there were 32 newspapers in her county—each circulating in her market area. Although she had lived in the area for 15 years, she had never heard of most of them. Many were small-circulation publications directed at special groups: ethnic or religious publications, women, business, singles, sports, etc. Each had survived long enough to prove that certain advertisers had found a happy home. Unless such publications produce results for advertisers, they go out of business. It is just that simple.

Jan's business opening was scheduled six weeks from the time she began to check into her advertising possibilities—not enough time to check them all. She chose six to look into: the weekly and daily that covered her community, and four others chosen because she had at least heard of them. She ruled out the large metropolitan daily because it had no special page or section for her area, and therefore no special rates for her.

Jan wrote down a list of questions to take with her to the advertising departments she planned to visit. She didn't depend upon her memory. She took a small notebook with her and carefully wrote down the answers to her questions for later comparison when she made her decision. She wrote down rates, special rates (declining rates for volume advertising), and what special help she could expect from the staff, such as graphics, layout, copy preparation. She also got some helpful advice on how to stretch her advertising dollars—plus some conflicting advice on how to plan her budget. She discounted some dubious advice as one business (the newspaper) trying to sell to another business (her). She was told her budget was too low (she knew this, but it was all she felt she could afford), and she was advised to put all her budget into the particular newspaper she happened to be investigating. She kept her objective firmly in mind—her own self-interest, as opposed to the newspaper's self-interest.

The small weekly Jan visited proved it had excellent coverage in her market area—over 80 percent of all the homes. Jan continued until she had investigated all the newspapers on her list, noting the locations of heaviest circulation in relation to her expectations of attracting customers. She went to the trouble of calling up several small advertisers in the papers and asking them their personal experience with advertising in the area, which newspaper pulled best for them. She found that other small business owners are eager to help a kindred soul and have much worthwhile advice to offer.

Armed with as much information as she could gather, Jan made her decision. She chose the larger daily for its wider coverage, because she figured that an antique shop must pull from a larger area than most other kinds of shops. She chose the solid hometown weekly with its saturation coverage, because she felt her steady customers would be the townspeople. Instead of choosing more newspapers for her opening ads, Jan saved some of her budget for radio and direct-mail advertising, and filed away the other four newspapers for future possibilities. She made a mental note to investigate each of the 32 newspapers in her area, on the grounds that she might be missing a potent source of customers if she didn't.

Jan's opening was a success. Since she knew nothing about preparing advertising copy, she accepted all the free help she could get from the ad departments of the local newspapers. Added to that, Jan hired a graphics artist to produce a logo for her shop. (A logo is a special design that identifies you or your business on sight.) In Jan's case, her logo was a three-legged iron kettle, a copy of a kettle she hung outside her shop door. She used the logo on her stationery, direct mail advertising, flyers, ads, and even on the receipts she gave customers. Soon, when her customers saw an envelope in their mail boxes with an iron kettle in the corner, they recognized Jan's shop. For the $150 she paid the artist to do the original design, Jan owned the symbol for life—a worthwhile investment, even though the $150 seemed a little stiff at the time she spent it.

Jan used the same ad in both newspapers and earmarked a quarter of her entire year's advertising budget for her first month in business. In addition, she made the most out of her opening publicity, combining publicity and advertising. Her opening was covered by both local newspapers, and about half of the other 30 newspapers ran the press release Jan sent them. She was the lead story in the region's business publication, which used her as an example of the dramatic increase of women setting up their own businesses. It was a good angle for the newspaper and a good story for Jan. Her business got off to a rousing start. A year later, she had passed a critical marker—still in business and still struggling, but with high hopes for a bright future.

SPECIALTY PUBLICATIONS

Each medium for advertising has its own characteristics. Newspapers with general circulations reach people of both sexes, all races, all ages, various income levels, and varied interests. Your daily or weekly newspaper is an overall good shotgun approach for you, but many businesses are gravitating toward combining a general approach with a specific one. Therefore, specialty publications are experiencing a boom period. If your business is patronized by few blacks, for example, and there are 10,000 blacks in your marketing area, it makes good business sense to seek out a publication which reaches blacks. The same is true for women, singles, divorced people, sports enthusiasts, racing fans, teenagers, and an array of others reached by specialty publications. Don't shrug off specialty newspapers until you investigate their circulations. You may be passing up a good, inexpensive way of reaching people who would be interested in becoming your customers.

Advertising rates for small publications, covering special groups, are usually low because of their low circulation. If a small newspaper reaches 1,000 paid subscribers, however, and you multiply this by three, you may have an excellent chance of getting a higher-than-average percentage of 3,000, depending upon how well your business fits with the readers. Specialty newspapers tend to have extremely loyal readers who make a special effort to patronize the publication's advertisers. And you can be sure your ad will be read, since the publication is so small that nothing escapes the reader.

No matter what ad department you visit, you will hear, over and over, that hit-and-miss advertising does not work— that advertising builds upon advertising, and recognition is gained through steady exposure. It may sound self-serving, but it's true. No matter what publication you choose, give it a fair trial of several months—a minimum of three. Give the readers a chance to get to know you. Many an advertiser is ready to quit in disgust when the first ad fails to bring one single phone call or new customer. Repetition builds recognition, which is the reason television ads drive you up the wall—repeating, repeating. As the ad drives you wild, it also imprints a product name in your brain which causes you to respond two days later as you stroll down the supermarket aisle. You may not make the connection, but those producing the advertising have.

Choose carefully when you decide on a specialty publication—but once chosen, clench your teeth and wait. You'll be wasting your money with one or two insertions. Don't advertise at all until you can afford a proper test. When you advertise in specialty newspapers, combine imaginative publicity with your ads. These small publications are receptive to good story ideas and may print your press releases which were turned down by larger newspapers. Although it's never ethical to tie editorial coverage to advertising, it is a fact of life that small newspapers (and big ones as well) look more favorably upon publicity from advertisers—especially publicity from business owners. If it's a good story, it will get printed anyway. But if it's a marginal story, being an advertiser may push it over the acceptable line. It's a thin, subtle line. (If it stops being thin and subtle and a small paper offers you a "deal," run to the nearest exit.)

Shopping Sheets

There are thousands of shopping sheets, mailed third-class to "Occupant," helping make up the mounds of "junk mail" which go into every home. They are light on editorial content and heavy on badly produced, cheap display and classified advertising.

Who reads them? Are they worthwhile for you to consider?

The answer depends entirely upon the success of any particular shopping sheet in any given area. Many of them are useless because they go from the mailbox to the trash can, but there are exceptions. Generally, the exceptions grow into small publications with more editorial content or into advertising mediums with no editorial content.

You'll have to use a different yardstick to measure effectiveness. For example, if you made a decision on the basis of circulation, combined with their very low rates, you'd jump at the chance to advertise. However, you must take into consideration that their circulation is unsolicited, and many times unwanted. A lot of "Occupants" wish they weren't so blessed. Any publication which circulates free is suspect. When people pay for a publication, it is a good indication they will read it. When they don't pay for it, and have no choice in whether they get it, the rules for deciding whether the publication is a good place to advertise change radically.

Until you can afford to take chances, pass such shopping sheets by. Unless, of course, there is one in your neighborhood read by everybody, including yourself and your neighbors. Ask other small business owners whose ads appear regularly. It could be one of those rare offbeat publications which reach many potential customers for a very few advertising dollars. It does happen, but not often.

Display and Classified Tabloids

Somebody explained it as the "attic instinct" that lurks in people; however, nobody knows for sure why so many people leaf through 40 pages of badly printed advertising copy week after week—but they do.

There has been a phenomenal rise in small tabloid-type formats in which a front page, a back page, and everything in between is covered with advertising. These tabloids fit every criteria for junk mail except one. People read them. They read them even though they are badly produced, badly printed, and haphazardly laid out, with everything from a two-line classified ad selling a pair of ice skates to a full page display ad from the supermarket.

Check your area before you leap, but many small businesses have found that advertising in these publications has produced results far exceeding expectations. One small business owner advertised in three newspapers and a "pennysaver" for the grand opening of a flower shop. She placed an identifiable coupon in all publications, and discovered that the pennysaver had drawn twice as many people as the three newspapers combined.

Rates in such publications are generally low, so if yours is the kind of business that might fit, try a small classified ad for several weeks. If it produces, go on to a small display ad. If the display ad fails to produce more than the classified ad—a distinct possibility—go back to the classified.

Business Newspapers

If yours is a business that sells to other businesses, such as a small public relations firm, by all means advertise in your area's business publication. You will reach an exclusive readership of business executives and others interested in business. If, however, your business is a fish store, it makes no sense to advertise in a business paper.

Regardless of what business you are in, it does make sense to become a reader of your business newspaper. You will find many helpful business tips, trends, and information you'll not find anywhere else.

When you're ready to hire help such as public relations, advertising, an answering service, management trainees, photographers, temporary office workers, etc., a business newspaper is a good place to look for specialized help.

RADIO ADVERTISING

Radio, at best, is fragmented—its audience separated and grouped. A station which plays classical music doesn't expect many teenage listeners. A station which plays rock-and-roll doesn't expect many adult listeners. An afternoon talk show may appeal primarily to unemployed people — senior citizens, housewives, shut-ins — while a news broadcast timed for homeward-bound commuters may draw from many groups.

Radio advertising can be effective and pinpointed to your needs. Certainly you should investigate radio advertising in your area if it's reaching your customers. Many small businesses have prospered with radio advertising to the point of sponsoring programs. Local radio rates are generally quite reasonable. For example, Jan's antique business might produce an interesting five-minute daily or weekly radio program, combining an interesting subject with advertising her wares.

On the other hand, a few radio commercials spread over several months is tossing advertising money to the winds, lost by attempting to reach people on a mass basis.

Broadcast audiences are harder to measure than print readers, though there are organizations which measure radio as there are with newspapers. Radio audiences are measured through samples of listeners, chosen to represent an average. The Broadcast Rating Council audits the major broadcast-measuring services to insure certain standards are used. What these surveys can tell you is the station's share of audience, broken down by sex, age, and other characteristics, plus the number of radios in your broadcast area. As with newspapers, rates go up in relation to the number of listeners.

Naturally, the trick is to match your potential customers to the radio audience. If you own a record shop selling heavily to teenagers, placing commercials on a rock-and-roll station may work fine. The same is true for other audiences. Learn as much as possible about the program's regular listeners and match them to your business.

For example, the owner of a small women's clothing store in an exclusive suburb which sold expensive brands at discount prices bought several one-minute commercials on a noontime program directed at women. The program host interviewed leaders of various volunteer and professional organizations and broadcast area events scheduled for the following weeks. The clothing owner's business picked up immediately. Finally, the radio commercials had increased her business so much the owner sponsored the entire 15-minute program. There are many similar success stories.

If you choose radio advertising, don't allow the charts and audience estimates to cloud your own judgment. Radio space salespersons are in business to get you to advertise as much as possible. Pick and choose carefully the times and the programs. Monitor your own commercials. If the station's copy department writes your commercials, make sure you edit them so that the final drafts say what you want said. Don't be afraid to insist on doing it your way and changing the commercials whenever you feel it is necessary. Accept all the advice and help the station can give you, but make all decisions. As with most small businesses, radio stations are notoriously understaffed, with one person doing three jobs. Unless you speak up, you'll get short shrift. Your thirty-second announcement could run five years unchanged unless you insist on a rewrite.

TELEVISION ADVERTISING

The cost of television advertising for the small business is generally prohibitive. Even the small local television station in medium-sized cities is too wide in coverage and too costly for most small businesses. However, there are exceptions in those areas with cable or UHF television. Here you may find rates competitive with other advertising media.

Investigate television with the same careful eye on audience charts as for radio. Find out who the viewers are and where they live—their sex, their age, and their income level. And even though rates are a bargain after midnight, don't waste your money buying time unless you're convinced your potential customers are insomniacs.

THE YELLOW PAGES

Does it make sense to advertise in the yellow pages? Yes, it does. Almost always, and for almost every business.

For example, if you are a plumber you'll get business calls on the basis of an individual's instant reaction to a clogged drain. A home-owner who hasn't needed a plumber in five years will remember the yellow pages long after the memory of your name vanishes. And a new resident will check the yellow pages for any number of services, including dentists, doctors, and lawyers. A small ad giving a little extra information about your business can give you an edge over your competitors who settle for the plain business listing.

Small local phone books with business advertising and special listings can also be good places to reach potential customers, if the local book replaces a large cumbersome phone book. How much these special phone books are used depends upon where you live. The choice must be yours.

GIMMICK ADVERTISING

In every home there are calendars, matchbooks, keychains, pencils, pens, notepads, shopping bags, drinking glasses, and various other items lumped together as gimmick advertising. Gimmick advertising has been around for years and has worked for many advertisers, else it would have died out long ago.

This type of advertising can be particularly successful in small communities where the local residents line up for their calendars and hang your business name and phone number (on the calendar) in their dens or kitchens. It works well for grand openings, special sales, or celebrations such as the bicentennial.

If you use gimmick advertising, try to come up with a clever idea—one which will get you an equivalent amount of publicity. Naturally, don't do something that will backfire, such as the pet shop which gave out live turtles and was called to task for cruelty to animals.

If your advertising budget is so low that a few hundred pencils will make a sizable dent, wait until you are more successful to engage in this type of advertising. Make up for it in good public relations. Save the gimmicks until you're on more solid financial ground.

THE SILVER SCREEN

Movies in many small towns and suburban areas solicit advertising from local merchants. A little multiplication—seats times showings times number of days advertising—will give you the maximum number of people it is possible for you to reach this way. Not many small businesses use movie advertising, but a few find it profitable. If teenagers in your area frequent a drive-in movie and the bulk of your sales come from them, you might find they react to your ad on the screen. If you do find that the movie advertising is for you, you'll be the exception. Most small businesses find it isn't worth the money.

BILLBOARD ADVERTISING

This highly specialized advertising works extremely well for certain businesses: hotels and motels, restaurants, recreational facilities, small unique shops buried in an area bypassed by a major highway. For example, there is a tiny factory outlet in a small West Virginia town which does a land-office business in expensive crystal strictly because of two billboards—one facing each way on a major highway.

Many small and large businesses have found billboard advertising profitable, since the country is covered with billboards. A lot of billboards have gone up since the first Burma Shave sign.

Check out your location in relation to network highways carrying their thousands of tourists. A well-placed billboard, cleverly designed with simple, clear directions to your door, could give you a big shot of adrenalin in the cash receipts. It has done it for others.

LOCAL TRANSPORTATION

The trains, buses, subways, and taxis in large cities are covered with advertising. In New York City you can even buy tee-shirt advertising on live models. Is this type of advertising helpful to the struggling small business?

Not unless you have a unique business or a budget that can stand a lot of experimenting. Advertisers on public transportation are usually larger businesses—banks, national products, Broadway plays in New York. Of course, if you are the owner of a small bus company or a fleet of taxis, make every effort to attract such advertisers. For the average small business, however, this type of advertising isn't worth it.

If you decide to run a political campaign, it works better—a lot of exposure for a short amount of time. If you have a small hardware store or a variety store, stick to the conventional media.

HIGH SCHOOL AND COLLEGE PUBLICATIONS

It's hard—practically impossible—for any small business person in a community to refuse an ad in the high school yearbook. So go ahead and advertise, but don't expect increased sales. The return of your investment will be in good will—a long-term investment.

A high school newspaper is another story. It's a good place for a record shop, a hamburger stand, a small electronics business, a bicycle shop, and dozens of other small businesses to advertise on a regular basis. Teenagers have a lot of money these days.

NINE

Creating an Ad

G ONE ARE THE DAYS WHEN ALL ADS RESEMBLED TODAY'S classifieds—short two-line announcements like: "Lost. Two hogs owned by Farmer Brown. Reward for return."

Today's ads range from a tiny do-it-yourself shopping-news display ad to a double-page, foldout, four-color, slick magazine ad which costs thousands of dollars and requires a team of experts to produce. It's not unusual to come upon a large, full-page metropolitan newspaper ad with little more copy than Farmer Brown wrote to get back his hogs. Most of the ad is devoted to white space framing copy. Occasionally you'll flip past an upside-down ad, or one using Chinese-type lettering, or a full page of microscopic copy without a single picture. Each different ad is trying out a new approach to grab your attention.

For the small advertiser, it's better to stick to tried and tested advertising methods rather than springing for fancy lettering and far-out messages. Today, as in the early days of advertising, simple, clear, direct advertising sells best. You're in business, and advertising is a selling tool of your trade. Use it with good taste, but don't try to disguise the fact that your advertising is meant to sell. Nothing is more infuriating than an ad so subtle it flies under false colors right up to the last revealing sales message. Whether this type of advertising is dishonest is not the point. The point is that the customer perceives it to be dishonest. Nobody wants to be had in an ad.

So let your advertising sell, openly and honestly, and forget words like *sensational, colossal, stupendous, greatest sale in history, world's best bargains,* and a host of other superlatives discounted as baloney by a bombarded public. Even if you could prove your sale is the world's greatest, nobody would believe you. And you are dealing with your customers' feelings and suspicions, regardless of hard facts.

The first rule in ad writing is brevity. Make it short. Never use a big word if a little word will do as well. Never use two adjectives to describe something if one does the job. Use simple sentences. Avoid using conjunctions such as *and, but, or, for,* to link thoughts. Use common words which everybody will understand. When you communicate with a large audience, you want your message to be understood by the least educated. Use words sparingly, leaving white space for eye appeal. Crowded ads are hard to read. Make your ads easy and comfortable to read.

YOUR COPY

Begin writing your ad copy by putting down a list of things that must be in the ad—things you cannot possibly leave out, such as:

- Your business name.
- Your address.
- Phone number.
- Merchandise, product, or service you're selling.

Already you've put down the skeleton of your copy. What's left is the creative part of the ad—that special appeal that will grab your readers and cause them to react in the way you want them to react.

Now add the missing ingredient:

- The conditions: What will make your ad come alive? A special sale? A special price? A special item? What are you offering that sets this ad apart from all others?

If the answer is nothing, you have more creativity ahead of you. Perhaps this is an image-building ad, that needs spicing up a little. Perhaps before you decide what copy to write you should familiarize yourself with the various types of ads which appear day after day in thousands of publications.

Announcement Ads

This type of ad merely states a fact. It is low-profile, soft-sell—avoiding any appearance of overt selling. Professional services often use the announcement-ad approach, merely listing location and service—a move to a different location, a new service.

Announcement ads are used by old, well-known, established firms to announce new divisional locations, new partners, and new products. Many small shops, such as clothing stores, use direct-mail announcements to alert charge customers to a special sale. They do this by mailing out flyers or postcards to their regular customers a few days before newspaper ads announce the sale. This approach motivates in two ways: It gives regular customers a feeling of getting special attention, and it says "Come and get it before the hordes of public customers appear." It creates an urgency for regular customers that otherwise would not be there, and it works successfully.

Reminder Ads

You see them all the time: School is just around the corner—Summer will arrive before you know it—The season for a cruise is upon us—Plant a garden—Get ready for winter—etc. An airline reminds us, in a creative ad, that every American has two heritages, so discover your other heritage by flying to Italy, Ireland, Germany, or Japan.

Reminder ads work well by reminding people of unpleasant things: Remember the icy roads last winter, so get snow tires early—Protect your family by buying a burglar alarm. In an area plagued by hurricanes, a storm-shutter retailer ran a hurricane disaster picture along with his sales message. It worked for him (but it didn't do much for the local real estate people).

Reminder ads give you a jumping-off point for writing your advertising copy, provide a subject to get you started. Fit reminder ads in with community events, special days, sporting events, vacation periods, school activities, community clubs, trips, local history, and dozens of other activities. Reminder ads work well for small businesses which have created their own special events. A cider mill gives free cider on opening day each year. The ad reminds customers to "Come and get your free cider." A marina in a small resort area reminds customers of reduced opening-week prices. A clothing retailer reminds customers of last year's August sale. The message: "A second chance this year."

Introductory Ads

Introductory ads, as the name implies, are used to introduce a product or service for the first time. Such ads are also used year after year to introduce a new wrinkle in an old idea—a new model car, a new, improved product, an old dogfood cut in small pieces for puppies.

If you overuse this kind of advertising, you're likely to kill its effectiveness, since it's unlikely you can introduce something new and different week after week. For a change of pace, introductory ads can create new business.

Copy for introductory ads must include more than the ordinary sales information. It must tell customers what's new about the service or product, why they need it, how they need it, and where they can find it. Your copy-writing creativity can sparkle here, since you have a job of persuasion to do. Will this product or service save time? Save money? Make you feel better? Look younger? Be happier?

Keep in mind that many consumers are weary of advertising that promises eternal health, happiness, and a secure love life through the purchase of a tube of toothpaste. One clever advertiser, however, turned this weariness into an advantage. He ran an introductory ad for a new product with a caption line: "Guaranteed *not* to improve your sex life . . . but . . ." It was an attention-getter where he used the misleading claims of others to focus attention on his product.

Bargain Ads

Price is the significant factor—the star—in a bargain ad. It can appeal to a consumer buying a $200,000 yacht as well as a shopper stocking up on soup at five cans for a dollar. Nearly everybody is interested in saving money, no matter how much money they earn or accumulate.

There are many ways to feature bargains. Extra service is a bargain, the same as two cents off on a can of peas. Think of all the things that are bargains: a smaller down payment, a layaway item with time payments that begin three months later; a special guarantee; free installation; free estimates, and a host of others. The sky (and your imagination) is the limit on your bargain ads.

Large and small department stores successfully run long lists of bargains, usually classified into separate sections such as furniture, children's clothing, etc., and list regular and sale prices. Sometimes such ads are done with a countdown approach—last two days of bargain sale; Monday-only bargains.

A number of cost-conscious businesses advertise that they won't be undersold by any competitor. If a customer brings in advertising proof of underselling, the first business matches the competitor's price.

This works well for discount stores or stores which always feature price as the single attraction. But it is risky for others. This kind of advertising can label you "cut-rate." Remember that customers flock to quality stores at sales times, buying the exact same items discount stores sell year round for the same price.

In a bargain ad, make sure you show the customer, through price comparison, that you are offering a bargain. Many people will never know otherwise. Most impulse buying occurs because the customer is led, through comparison, to the bargain. The bargain instinct is alive and well in most people, even those who claim to be unaffected. Many an attic or basement is filled with "bargains" sold in December and discarded before June.

One man, known to his friends as Mr. Consumer, is kidded because he will buy anything that plugs into an electric outlet. His basement is filled with "bargains" he couldn't resist—kitchen appliances, tools, lighting fixtures, electric toothbrushes, and scalp massagers. For Christmas, a friend who is a small business owner gave him a potato masher with a phony wired-on electric cord. It was a good joke that made the point, but it didn't stop Mr. Consumer. He goes his merry way, delighting small and large businesses. He's not the only one. Just about every second person you meet is a bargain-hunter. Make it easy for them to find yours.

IMAGE-BUILDING

Whether you realize it or not, your weekly or monthly advertising builds an image—a mental picture which sticks like flypaper. It can help you if it is the right kind of image, but it can hurt you if it isn't.

For example, think of full-page, drug-store-type ads where item after item is listed, each with a huge dollar sign. There's not an eighth of an inch of white space, and huge black letters proclaim "Gigantic Savings." "Junk" is what comes into a lot of consumers minds—cheap, cut-rate, low quality, no-guarantee, no-service, no-return junk, not worth carrying out of the store if it were offered free.

There are many "junk" places in business strictly because they buy and sell low-quality merchandise. But for thousands of small businesses, this is not the kind of image that builds loyal customers who trust you and your goods or services—the kind of customer who pays the rent and keeps you in business.

From the day you open your doors for business, your image builds. If you are in control of your image instead of your image being in control of you, those characteristics of which you are most proud will be what builds your image.

When you compete on the wrong terms, you build a wrong image. For example, many a small business owner has gone out of business because of trying to compete with big businesses the wrong way. Compete on your own terms—not on theirs. If you own a fine grocery that delivers and you are located near a giant supermarket, don't fight it out on price. Advertise service, quality, loyalty, personal attention, length of time in the community, smallness. Build a solid image featuring the special aspects of your business. There is something every small business can do better than any other small (or large) business. Discover your uniqueness and build your image around it. If you cannot find anything unique, create something.

For example, there is a small country grocery with a unique display of tools, kitchen appliances, and other items used in the same store a century ago. It traces the history of the retail grocery business through the various generations of one family. It offers tours and lectures to local schoolchildren, and has become a landmark in the community. Within a ten-mile radius of this small grocery, a dozen giant supermarkets coexist.

If you don't build an image, it will grow anyway—sometimes into a monster which can destroy you.

CHOOSING TYPE

You needn't know anything about the history of printing or such terms as Roman, Gothic, Italic, and Sans Serif, to be able to choose eye-appealing type for your ads. Leaf through magazines and newspapers, noting the various kinds of type used. Which is easiest for you to read? Which is the most attractive? What combinations did you find pleasing?

Occasionally a novelty type can be used to good advantage but the best type to use, generally, is the kind of type that is easiest to read. This is generally type that is most familiar to the general public.

In choosing the typeface and copy content of your ads, there are some guidelines to consider. There are no hard-and-fast rules, since for every rule there is someone who has successfully broken it. Generally, however:

- Choose familiar, easy-to-read type, and steer clear of fancy lettering, vertical, and/or flush-right printing.

This is *flush left, justified type:*

Justified type is used for
newspaper columns or pages
of books. Each line comes
out exactly the same size,
measured automatically by
the linotype machine used.

This is *flush left, with ragged right edge:*

This block of type is set flush left
with the right edge allowed to
fall within a four- or five-letter
space limit. This type is familiar because most typewritten material is flush
left, with ragged right edge.

Stepped lines:

Stepped lines are set the same width,
   with each line moved to the right by
      a set increment. It probably is not
         worth the time it takes to space out.

Novelty approach:

A
good
way to
think of
friends at
Christmas is
with a special
gift certificate from
EILEEN'S GIFTS.
Special sale to begin
this Thursday. Clip out
coupon below for bargains.
Sale ends at 6 P.M. Xmas Eve.
So come one and come all. 'Tis
the season to be merry. Refresh-
ments from 3 P.M. until 6 P.M.
Sale ends
Christmas
Eve at
6 P.M.

Even though the type is hard to read, the figure outlined by the type is familiar. Any novelty approach should be accompanied by clear, easy-to-read type somewhere else in the ad.

Flush right:

This kind of typesetting is the
opposite of flush left. It's not
familiar to the reader and forces
the reader to search for the start
of every line.

Vertical lines:

V	l	a	t
e	i	r	o
r	n	e	
t	e		r
i	s	h	e
c		a	a
a		r	d
l		d	

- Use hand lettering sparingly, since it is harder to read than familiar type.
- Choose your type and stick to it. Repeated use will build recognition.
- Use the largest type possible in your ads without crowding.
- Don't set type too wide. It will be hard to read.
- Don't set type too narrow. It crowds.
- Use capital letters sparingly. They are harder to read than lower case.
- Use white space generously.
- Use combinations of types sparingly. Too many typefaces will detract from the ad's contents.

USING ARTWORK

Artwork has three main functions in your ad:

- To explain or demonstrate a product or service.
- To get the attention of the reader.
- To improve the ad's appearance and create a receptive mood in the buyer.

There are three main sources for artwork:

- Photography.
- Hand art.
- Professional services.

Photography

If you're the captain of a fishing charter boat, the best way to interest prospective customers is to use a picture of a fish you caught this season, the bigger the better. Even if Michelangelo could return and sketch a fish, a photograph of the real thing would sell your product better. Photographs leave no room for doubt. They are instantly believed. Generally the closer to home a photograph is taken, the greater the interest by the public. A picture of a prize-winning tomato in your neighbor's garden would interest you. But if it were growing in your own garden it would generate more interest. Generally, people are interested, first in themselves, next in those closest to them, and last, in those farthest away. Anytime you can link a service or product to a local person or event through photographs, do it.

Naturally you can't afford the rates of a top professional photographer, but there is a lot of photographic help you can afford. The local newspaper photographer may do free-lance work for reasonable rates or may be able to recommend a talented amateur. You may find an amateur in a high school or college photography class. Ask a camera shop owner. There are dozens of shutter-switchers anxious to display their wares. Find one or two and keep their phone numbers for special assignments.

The distributors of lines you handle supply photographs. Many times these will work in with your ads, and they are free for the asking.

Hand Art

Most small advertisers expect sketches and paintings to be too expensive to even ask about. Chances are there are inexpensive artists in your own neighborhood wishing you'd call. Why local high school or college students don't get together with local advertisers for mutual benefit is a mystery. A local high school student's artwork in an ad, with an identifying credit line, will be read regardless of the ad's professionalism. It will also be clipped out, discussed in class, and immortalized in scrapbooks. Art teachers are generally delighted to take on assignments of specific artwork for ads.

There are also young, inexpensive artists who are beginning careers, grateful for the exposure your ads will give them. Find them through your local newspaper, art teachers, art supply stores, or through a classified ad.

Art can be used in ads to illustrate points in advertising copy and to explain how products are to be used. Art can create a feeling of luxury and satisfaction that cannot be matched by photography. There are advantages to artwork, especially in fashion ads, hair styling, and for business that is connected with art products. Use hand art sparingly, but use it.

Professional Artwork Services

Professional artwork services—if you consider buying directly—are prohibitively expensive for the small advertiser. But when you use them as most advertiser do —through your newspaper—they are free, supplied by the newspaper's advertising department as part of its service to you. Without these advertising aids, newspapers would be forced to triple their creative staffs several times over.

These professional services supply huge, heavy books with page after page of indexed illustrations which can be clipped and used in your ads. Each illustration is numbered so as to avoid duplication with other ads. These services were once called mat services, before most newspapers converted to offset printing. Molten lead was poured into heavy mats, and the mold was used to print the illustration. Now, all that's necessary to produce camera-ready copy is to clip out an illustration and paste it on the ad layout sheet.

FREE HELP WITH YOUR ADS

At this point, you may want to continue producing your own ads, but bear in mind that most small business owners don't—for good reasons. Part of a newspaper's service to you is the preparation of your ads, from the first word of copy to the last illustration, as long as you're willing to settle for what their advertising department offers. What most newspapers generally offer is complete layouts and finished copy, combining the artwork they buy from artwork services with some simple handwork such as line sketches.

Small newspapers seldom employ professional artists, but most people who have worked in advertising departments for a while perform some of the same functions, and often do a creditable job with your requests. They won't take special photographs for you but will work with your photographs, cropping, fitting, and integrating them into your ad.

The small advertiser who puts himself or herself into the hands of an advertising manager is well off if the manager is a conscientious, dedicated professional with the time to devote to his or her special problems. A great many fit this criterion, for the simple reason that the health of your business is the backbone of their business. A newspaper advertising representative is delighted to help you grow from a tiny advertiser into a big advertiser.

However, it is possible to run into an ad salesperson more interested in getting your signature on an advertising contract than in helping your business. You may get in over your head financially, and get canned instead of creative advertising after you're signed up. The only way to avoid these pitfalls is through careful investigation and eternal vigilance after the contract is signed. The more you know about the advertising business, the more you will be able to use a newspaper's advertising assistance to your best advantage. A good advertising manager will welcome your knowledge and will work with you to make your business succeed. His or her advice will be invaluable.

WORKING WITH YOUR NEWSPAPER

Unless your newspaper has an advertising staff which is permanently out to lunch, it will save you time, trouble, and money to use their assistance. But stay on top of your own advertising. Make suggestions. Talk about new ideas and ways to make your ads sell better. You'll find your help will be valued by newspaper advertising professionals.

"I have enormous respect for the judgment and knowledge of the small business person," says Advertising manager John Gallian, who works with 1200 small businesses in the 160-mile stretch of the Florida Keys covered by the Florida Keynoter in Marathon. "They know their business better than anybody else, and they have first-rate ideas for promoting it. But my greatest difficulty as an advertising manager is getting information from small business owners—information valuable in making their own businesses successful."

Accept suggestions from the professionals, but run your own show. When you get a new idea, discuss it early. You may discover it can't be done mechanically, or the cost will be prohibitive, or the timing conflicts with other events coming up in the community. There are thousands of considerations which can affect your advertising. In considering the possibility of some calamity, keep in mind the old saying about advertising: "If anything bad can happen, it will."

COOPERATIVE ADVERTISING

Cooperative advertising is cost-sharing between a manufacturer and a retailer for mutual benefits. Certain retailers shun cooperative advertising because of the headaches and paperwork involved in performance contracts. Others use it beneficially. Since the advertising funds are there for the asking, you should investigate whether it will work for you.

Rules for cooperative advertising are laid down by the individual manufacturers, generally covering a lengthy period—a year or more—during which retailers agree to advertise the manufacturer's products. In actual practice, retailers cannot collect until the ads are run and proof submitted of contract performance—no proof, no pay. There are other special deals offered by manufacturers, such as allowances for displays and promotions.

Ask your local advertising manager if his or her services include assistance with cooperative advertising. If so, you're in luck. If not, investigate cooperative advertising yourself. And have your lawyer look over any contract before you sign it. Get specific answers to the following:

- The percentage or amount it will cost you.
- Exactly how and when you will be reimbursed.
- What, if any, restrictions on the kind of media used.
- What proof the manufacturer requires for reimbursement, such as invoices, proof sheets, etc.

According to one newspaper advertising manager, "Thousands of dollars which could be used by small advertisers lie waiting for the asking." Make sure you ask.

Direct Mail

T HOUSANDS OF SMALL BUSINESS OWNERS HAVE FOUND direct mail to be the least expensive (per sale) and most effective way of reaching their customers.

Generally speaking, the smaller your business, the more effective direct mail becomes—although direct mail is not limited to small business by any means. It is used widely and successfully by big and small business.

Direct mail advertising and publicity offers you the ultimate in selectivity. You alone decide precisely who is to receive your messages. If you want to, you can reach potential customers on the basis of any number of qualifiers: sex, race, age, occupation, education, special interest, religion, marital status, and residence. Instead of a shotgun approach, you can narrow the target to your satisfaction. You can mail to a city block or to the entire state. You're in complete control, and you can do whatever is effective.

Whatever you do in direct mail promotion, there are three rules:

- Make it short.
- Make it clear.
- Make it count.

As business has become more and more specialized, the use of direct mail promotion has increased. Back in the days of the hitching post and the general store, there was no need to advertise—direct mail or any other way. Even the location was spread by word of mouth. But the old general store has been broken into smaller and smaller pieces: a cheese shop, tiny ethnic groceries, candy shops, notion stores, newspaper stands, hardware stores. Even the pieces have been broken into smaller pieces: an imported cheese shop; a textbook, instead of a general, bookstore; a restaurant serving only omelettes; tall men's and short men's shops; handmade Indian jewelry and African art—thousands of small, specialized businesses reaching out to specific customers through direct mail.

YOUR MAILING LIST

The day you open for business is the ideal time to begin your mailing list. From that moment forward, never miss an opportunity to add a name, update an address, include the friend of a friend. Two names a day add up to quite a list in ten years—or for that matter, six months. Your list will require dedication, because unless you keep it up-to-date it will become useless. Your list will be well worth your effort and will pay off in handsome profits, established customers, and a surefire way of instant contact. The owner of a small shop emerged from his burning building holding only a box in his hands. Even though it was the dead of winter, he had not stopped to grab his coat. All he took was his mailing list. He was a smart businessman. He could buy another coat.

Many successful businesses keep a ledger out front and ask customers to sign up. A few try to hide what they are doing by calling it a "guest book," an unnecessary deception. There's nothing wrong with collecting a mailing list. Be direct and honest in your approach. Explain exactly what the list is to be used for. Most people will be glad to add their names. Your established customers are eager to hear from you.

Compiling Your List
In addition to asking customers to sign up directly, there are many sources in your community from which you can draw a mailing list, including the following:

- Professional organizations and trade directories published and updated annually.
- Church memberships, clubs, service organizations, libraries. Some organizations sell or rent their mailing lists as a fund-raising means.
- Telephone directories, especially the local ones.
- Town hall records, such as building permits. (Town records are public information.)
- Newspaper listings of births, weddings, engagements.
- Local/national credit ratings.
- Commercial mailing lists compiled by those in the direct mail business. (For a fee you can have all or part of your direct mailing taken over.)
- Exchange lists. Many times your noncompetitive business associates will exchange lists with you.

Organizing Your List

Since postage is no longer a minor expense of small business, you may want to organize your lists into active and nonactive customers. Keep your system simple. If you keep several lists, code them for easy recognition, such as color coding. Make sure the slowest member of your business team can understand your system, or it will end up as a tangled mess wasting your long hours of hard work.

Check any list you have bought or exchanged and weed out duplications. Sending the same customer three direct mailing pieces gives the impression that your business is not too well organized, which is true. In keeping your list up-to-date, the job can be made easier if you:

- Mail out a perforated double post card annually asking that the customer mail back half with corrected name and address. Guarantee postage.
- Doublecheck changed names and/or addresses in your accounts receivable and also change them in your mailing list.
- Ask your sales staff to print—not write—names of customers. Stress accuracy.
- Watch newspapers for deaths, marriages, out of town moves. Sending notices to deceased persons is a painful experience for the family and the pain will be associated with you.

Miss, Mrs., or Ms.

Many established businesses are using Ms. to identify all women, regardless of their marital status. The reasons are obvious. It saves time—which is money—and is simple and easy to do.

It used to be a social blunder for any business to send mail to a newly married woman which addressed her as Miss. Until death—his, not hers—she was to be addressed by her husband's name, Mrs. John Jones. At his death she got back the first part of her name and, according to Emily Post, her socially correct mail must immediately change to Mrs. Mary Jones. To add to the confusion, many widows objected to the change, since to strip them of the name immediately upon death added to their grief. It was a complicated nightmare for the small business owner using direct mail.

By using Ms., it is possible to make some women angry if they prefer being called Mrs., but it is just as possible to make others angry by calling them Mrs. when they prefer being referred to as Ms. Since it is an even-up situation, more and more businesses are opting for Ms. The White House is no exception, except when sending mail to Mr. and Mrs.

COST OF DIRECT MAIL

Direct mail, in terms of return, can be the least expensive way to advertise, but not in the initial cost. In direct mail, as well as any kind of advertising, keep in mind that the true cost is in the return. A ten-dollar ad which returns nothing is a 100-percent loss. To get a rough idea of your direct mailing costs, add up the following and divide by the number of direct mailing pieces for the cost per mailing piece:

- Mailing costs (check weights carefully) per piece.
- Paper costs (envelopes and contents).
- Cost of preparation of contents: your time, employees' time, etc.
- Any extra costs, such as printing, typing, artwork.
- Delivery—mailing or hand delivery.

First Class or Cut Rate

Can you save money mailing third class, or should you go first class all the way? First class costs more, but it will get there sooner and give you any added prestige edge that comes with first class. Some people discard unopened third-class (junk) mail. Nobody does that to first class. Even though third class is slower and less predictable, you may be able to control this by sending it earlier. Third class is less impressive, but will that matter?

It depends upon you, your business, and the image you are trying to create with your customers. In many towns, third class is as good as first class. And a logo takes care of the identification problem by letting the receiver know instantly who the sender is. If you are clearly identified with your direct mail customers and they are pleased to hear from you, go with third class and save yourself a bundle. But if you are mailing to prospective customers and trying to garner new customers, go with first class.

In either first class or third class, don't squander your postage weight limits. Enclose flyers with your monthly bills or your own publicity to your customers. Most large department stores take full advantage of the extra space in direct mail. When have you opened a bill without finding an invitation to buy something else? If it's good business for the big stores, it is good business for the little ones. It's a way to make every penny count.

DIRECT MAILING CONTENTS

Here are some suggestions from the Small Business Administration* on the dangers to avoid in direct mail and some things to include:

Direct mail, like all other advertising, must be well done to be effective. Perhaps it has even more dangers than other forms of advertising, any one of which can sharply reduce its effectiveness. If you have experimented unsuccessfully with direct mail, any of the following hazards may have been the cause. In order to be successful your direct mail must:

1. Be sent to a select list of customers and prospects who can be given strong reasons for coming to your store. This list must be kept accurate and up-to-date. (Remember that *one out of five families,* on the average, will move every year.)

---

* U.S. Small Business Administration, *Small Marketers Aids,* No. 72, 1974.

2. The sales message which you send to them must tell them "what they want to hear," or *benefits* which they will gain from shopping with you.

3. Your sales message must be personal.

4. The mailing must fit the personality of your store, the merchandise or services advertised, and the people to whom it is addressed.

5. Each piece must be a selling piece. "Ask for the order"—try to get the reader to buy a specific item so you can measure the apparent selling effectiveness of it.

In addition, you may want to experiment further with your mailings and see if improved results justify the increased cost. For example, you might try: different grades and weights of paper; different printing processes; postcards, letters, pamphlets, or broadsides; individually addressed mail or simply "Occupant"; use of good illustrations or straight copy; price appeals, quality appeals, service appeals, or convenience features. Other advertisers have found significant variations in the pulling power of their direct mail with changes such as these.

Types of Direct Mail Advertising

Types of direct mail vary from a postcard, hand-written and hand-addressed, to the thousand-page, four-color mail-order catalog. In between these two come the more common forms in which you will be most interested—bulletins, pamphlets, letters, and so forth.

Any mailing may be used in any of three ways:

A single mailing to a single list of prospects (for making important announcements such as introducing new lines or new personnel, or a special promotion or short-term sale);

A short sequence of five or six mailings designed to sell a single offer (essentially a repetition of a basic proposition, with each mailing attracting a decreasing share of mailing addressees); or

A continuing series of regularly scheduled mailings weekly, semi-monthly, or monthly (a sustained campaign to the same mailing list with a different sales story in each mailing—very satisfactory for "neighborhood" stores where use of other advertising is impossible or impracticable).

The following are widely used programs which you may find suitable for your type of selling.

1. *Regular weekly mailing.* You can use this approach at times when newspaper advertising is impractical for some reason (more circulation than you need, as in metropolitan areas, or less circulation than you need, as in some small communities.)

This mail piece often resembles the newspaper advertisements of the large stores. You have to keep this presentation fresh and interesting. It must have some attention-getting "specials," and it must be timely.

It must also emphasize the reasons why a customer should come to *your* store. You should stress such factors as: convenient location, friendly atmosphere, plentiful parking, charge account, famous brands, and any special services you offer.

You can mimeograph this type of mail piece. You may want to distribute it door-to-door rather than mailing it as bulk mail. Either way, you can reach each family with a weekly message which you have tailored to tempt them into your store or service establishment. However, it seems that more people read the advertisement if you mail it.

Once you start this program and your customers come to depend on it, you should continue it or you may lose any patronage which your weekly ads have generated.

2. *Coupon mailing.* This is a powerful, short-term, special-event type of promotion. It is especially good for such occasions as grand openings, remodelings, the addition of a new department, or the introduction of a new feature or service.

It is a letter telling customers and prospects of the news and inviting them to visit your store for further details. It can be sent as bulk mail.

You add a coupon which offers something free—or at a reduced price—to bring the reader into your store. It can be a single coupon for a "one-shot" promotion. Here the coupon value must be substantial if it is to attract to the store a high percentage of your readers. Some people feel it is better to make this value "too good" rather than to err on the side of making it "not good enough."

Coupon promotions may wear themselves out if overused. It is better to use them sparingly—with really good values each time—than to attempt to use them too often with small values on the coupons.

For grand openings you may want to use the following variation. Mail out a series of three or four coupons, each one dated for use during a single week. Experience shows that customers will save such coupons (if they are of real value) for as long as three or four weeks. They will come in during the correct week to cash the coupon.

This technique helps prospects to form the habit of returning to your store week after week. It is expensive, so you have to regard it as an investment for building future business.

Be sure to send this kind of promotion to every family in your market area. Don't risk offending your regular customers by omitting them.

3. *Special letters.* This is one of the most valuable uses of direct mail advertising. It permits you to talk to a particular type of prospect with comparatively little waste circulation. For example, you can send a spe-

cial letter addressed to the parents of every new baby born in your market area. You personalize the special letter by addressing it to the individual instead of sending it as bulk mail.

You can send a letter to every new person who moves into your market area, inviting him or her to visit your store or service establishment. Here you can include a "get acquainted" offer.

You can use special letters to introduce new members of your organization and other changes, such as adding night shopping hours. Of course, they are cheaper if they are sent as bulk mail. In such a general announcement you do not need the first-class postage touch which is required when you write to one segment of your customers or prospects, such as parents of new babies.

4. *Other important mailings.* You can use direct mail advertising to sell to special groups. For example, you can send a single announcement of a special item to the members of a lodge, a fraternity, a church, a women's club, or a men's service club. Or you can advertise items which are needed and wanted by groups such as: doctors, dentists, lawyers, ministers, schoolteachers, and residents on rural routes.

These prospective customers can become an exceedingly profitable portion of your total business, if you will develop them in this way. You can find items in your store which are especially appropriate for these special groups. Or, by investigating, you may discover items which these groups would buy from you, if you stocked them and promoted them to each group *by direct mail.*

KEEP CHECKING

If your direct mail isn't working so well for you, check it carefully. Are your lists up-to-date? Are your mailings regular enough to build an image? Are you offering the right enticement? Have you used imagination and creativity in your messages? Do your customers understand your message? If so, are they responding in the way you want them to respond?

Until you can answer yes to all of the above questions, your direct mail promotion is not being utilized to its maximum. Keep writing different lyrics until your cash register sings.

ELEVEN

Measuring Advertising and Publicity

Expectations / Measuring Attitude Promotion

T HE CHAIRMAN OF THE BOARD OF A HUGE CORPORATION, which spends millions of dollars on advertising and publicity, admitted that half his budget produced no results. Absolutely nothing. Wasted. Squandered.

"So why don't you cut your budget in half?" asked a simple soul.

"Because I don't know which half is producing and which half isn't," was the chairman's answer.

This is true for large and small alike, but it's less of a problem for the small business owner than the chairman of a large corporation. Keeping track of the entire country is more complicated than counting heads in a small town or community, even though the principle remains the same. You've spent your promotion money and you'd like to know what it produced for you.

A simplistic notion is that good advertising produces increased sales and bad advertising does the reverse. It is generally true, but not always. Take for example the cranberry scare a few years back. All the advertising money in creation poured into promoting cranberries wouldn't have reversed a falling market. Circumstances can play a role, so before you decide on the worth of promotion, assess those circumstances which might have created a separate reaction—good or bad.

EXPECTATIONS

Essentially, measuring results means that you are measuring promotion dollars against sales increases. Promotion dollars include your time, which could have been spent doing something else—maybe more important—rather than producing promotion, so don't forget to include it.

In projecting your expectations, it is easier to divide promotion into the two basic kinds: that which you expect to produce immediate results, and the kind you expect to take longer, such as attitude promotion, your long-range image.

Immediate Response

This is planned in order to motivate a customer to buy a particular product or service within a short time—a day, a weekend, two weeks. For example, Christmas promotion is designed to produce results in a given time. On January 1st, after all the returns, you can get an accurate measurement of the success of your Christmas promotion.

Other examples might be clearance sales, special purchases, 24-hour sales. Since all promotion has some carryover effect—no matter when it is done—it is a good idea to recheck two or three weeks after your initial measurement. This kind of measurement is simple arithmetic, and comparisons can be extremely useful as years go by.

Take into consideration extraordinary circumstances which added or detracted—such as the cranberries. If you had a bumper Christmas season while others around you scraped by, congratulate yourself for unusual accomplishment. But if everybody is harvesting a bumper crop, your promotion may not be anything special—circumstances might have saved it.

Image Promotion

To a certain degree, all promotion falls into the category of image-building, whether you planned it that way or not. Attitude promotion is harder to measure, because concepts are more difficult to measure than dollars. It is tricky to measure your reputation. Sometimes your best friends won't tell you that your reputation has slipped. It's too personal for them to discuss, helpful though it may be to you if they did. You alone must be constantly on guard.

Attitude building is a steady process, created by the constant triggering of impulse to follow recognition. Long after a promotion, relationship can be established. For example, a promotion which announces that you have a new product or service pays off after customers have become convinced that they want that particular product or service and none other. This kind of attitude promotion lingers long, the message finally getting through the initial customer inertia or distrust.

"Why do you shop at that market when you could get the same things for less money down the street?" a housewife is asked.

It is because an attitude has developed in her mind about the kind of place she wants to do her marketing. She cannot be taken for granted, however, because your competitors are bombarding her with enticing offers. She will be far less likely to follow their suggestions if her image of you remains bolstered month after month. She needs to be reassured over and over again that her choice is sound, otherwise she may begin the recognition process with somebody else.

MEASURING ATTITUDE PROMOTION

Whether you are trying to measure attitude promotion on a short-term or long-term basis, work out points you can check against in following your promotion. The success of measurement, like everything else, requires some forethought in planning. In a small marketers aids series, here are some helpful suggestions on measuring promotional results, published by the Small Business Administration:*

Planning for Results
Whether you are trying to measure immediate response or attitude advertising, your success will depend on how well the ads have been planned. The trick is to work out points against which you can check after customers have seen or heard the advertisement.

Certain things are basic to planning advertisements whose results can be measured. First of all, *advertise products or services that have merit in themselves.* Unless a product or service is good, few customers will

---

* U.S. Small Business Administration, *Small Marketers Aids,* No. 121, 1976.

make repeat purchases, no matter how much advertising the store does.

Many people will not make an initial purchase of a shoddy item because of doubt or unfavorable word-of-mouth publicity. The ad that successfully sells inferior merchandise usually loses customers in the long run.

Small marketers, as a rule, *should treat their messages* seriously. Humor is risky as well as difficult to write. Be on the safe side and tell people the facts about your merchandise and services.

Another basic element in planning advertisements is to know *exactly what you wish a particular ad to accomplish.* In an immediate response ad, you want customers to come in and buy a certain item or items in the next several days. In attitude advertising, you decide what attitude you are trying to create and plan each individual ad to that end. In a small operation, the ads usually feature merchandise rather than store policies.

Plan the ad around only one idea. Each ad should have a single message. If the message needs reinforcing with other ideas, keep them in the background. If you have several important things to say, use a different ad for each one and run the ads on succeeding days or weeks.

The pointers which follow are designed to help you plan ads so they will make your store stand out consistently when people read or hear about it.

Identify your store fully and clearly. Logotypes or signatures in printed ads should be clean-lined, uncluttered, and prominently displayed. Give your address and telephone number. Radio and television announcements to identify your sponsorship should be full and as frequent as possible without interfering with the message.

Pick illustrations which are all similar in character. Graphics—that is, drawings, photos, borders, and layout—that are similar in character help people to recognize your advertising immediately.

Pick a printing typeface and stick to it. Using the same typeface or the same audio format on radio or television helps people to recognize your ads. Also using the same sort of type and illustrations in all ads allows you to concentrate on the message when examining changes in response to ads.

Make copy easy to read. The printed message should be broken up with white space to allow the reader to see the lines quickly.

Use coupons for direct mail advertising response as often as possible. Coupons give an immediate sales check. Key the coupon in some manner so that you can measure the response easily.

Get the audience's attention in the first 5 seconds of the radio and TV commercial. Also, get your main message in the first sentence if possible.

Tests for Immediate Response Ads

In weighing the results of your *immediate* response advertisements, the following devices should be helpful:

Coupons brought in. Usually these coupons represent sales of the product. When the coupons represent requests for additional information or contact with a salesman, were enough leads obtained to pay for the ad? If the coupon is dated, you can determine the number of returns for the first, second, and third weeks.

Requests by phone or letter referring to the ad. A "hidden offer" can cause people to call or write. Include—for example, in the middle of a paragraph—a statement that on request the product or additional information will be supplied. Results should be checked over a 1-week through 6-months or 12-months period, because this type ad may have considerable carry-over effect.

Split runs by newspapers. Prepare two ads (different in some way you would like to test) and run them on the same day. Identify the ads—in the message or with a coded coupon—so you can tell them apart. Ask customers to bring in the ad or coupon. When you place the ad, ask the newspaper to give you a split run—that is: to print "ad A" in part of its press run and "ad B" in the rest of the run. Count the responses to each ad.

Sales made of particular item. If the ad is on a bargain or limited-time offer, you can consider that sales at the end of 1 week, 2 weeks, 3 weeks, and 4 weeks came from the ad. You may need to make a judgment as to how many sales came from display and personal selling.

Check store traffic. An important function of advertising is to build store traffic which results in purchases of items that are not advertised. Pilot studies show, for example, that many customers who were brought to the store by an ad for a blouse also bought a handbag. Some bought the bag in addition to the blouse, others instead of the blouse.

You may be able to use a local college or high school distributive education class to check store traffic. Class members could interview customers as they leave the store to determine: (1) which advertised items they bought, (2) what other items they bought, and (3) what they shopped for but did not buy.

Testing Attitude Advertising

When advertising is spread out over a selling season or several seasons, part of the measurement job is keeping records. Your aim is comparing records of ads and sales for an extended time.

An easy way to set up a file is by marking the date of appearance on tear sheets of newspaper ads, log reports of radio and television ads, and copies of direct mail ads. The file may be broken down into monthly, quarterly, or semiannual blocks. By recording the sales of the advertised items on each ad or log, you can make comparisons.

In attitude (or image-building) advertising, the individual ads are building blocks, so to speak, which make up your advertising over a selling season. The problem is trying to measure each ad and the effects of all of the ads taken together.

One approach is making your comparisons on a weekly basis. If you run an ad, for example, each week, at the end of the first week after the ad appears, compare that week's sales with sales for the same week a year ago. At the end of the *second* week, compare your sales with those of the end of the first week as well as year-ago figures.

At the end of the *third* week, 1 month, 3 months, 6 months, and 12 months from the appearance of the ad, repeat the process, even though additional ads may have appeared in the meantime. For each of these ads, you will also make the same type of comparisons. You will, of course, be measuring the "momentum" of all of your ads as well as the results of a single ad.

After a time, you probably will be able to estimate how much of the results are due to the individual ad and how much to the momentum of all of your advertising. You may then make changes in specific details of the ad to increase response.

When comparing sales increases over some preceding period, allowances must be made for situations that are not normal. For example, your experience may be that rain on the day an ad appears cuts its pulling power by 50 percent. Similarly, advertising response will be affected by the fact that your customers work in a factory that is out on strike.

Some of the techniques which you can use for keeping on top of and improving attitude advertising follow:

Repeat

Repeat an ad. If response to an ad is good, run it—without change—two or three times and check the responses of each appearance against previous appearances.

Keep repeating the process. Much advertising loses effectiveness because the advertiser doesn't keep reminding people. Repetition helps increase knowledge of, and interest in, the product. You can soon estimate how often you should repeat each ad—exactly or with minor changes.

Analyze all ads in relation to response. Divide ads into at least two classes: high-response ads and low-response ads. Then look for differences between the two classes.

The time the ad was run may be responsible for a particular response level. Other factors, however, may be just as much or more influential than time. Consider the feature subject used in the illustration, persons shown, activities shown, types of merchandise, settings or backgrounds, different colors used. Also consider the message and how well it was expressed. Did the copy stick to the theme? Or did it wander? If slogans were used, did they help make the point?

Graphic elements may be important. Check to see which response category is associated with the presence of coupons, borders, display lines, small or incidental illustrations. Check response in relation to any variation in the way each appears. Compare any differences in type size and design or the boldness of the type.

Emphasis on brand names should also be checked. Price figures should be analyzed. If price lines are involved either in the ad or in the merchandise line of which the advertised product is a part, you should consider them also.

Check the size of the ad. It usually has a bearing on response. As a general rule, the larger the ad, the greater the response.

Try to see a pattern of dominance. Your analysis of high-and-low response ads may show that certain details—such as certain picture subjects—make the difference between a high or low response. Try to find the combinations which work best for your firm and merchandise.

Note changes occurring over time. A small retailer should never take a winning combination for granted. There is no single formula that will insure high response ads every time. Advertising changes. Therefore, you should watch the ads of others to see what changes are occurring. Continue to analyze your own ads, make small changes occasionally, and note any variations in response.

Listen to what people say about your ads. In doing so, try to discover the mental framework within which any comment about your ad was made. Then try to find points which reinforce believability and a feeling that your product fulfills some wish or need.

However, you should not be misled by what people say. An ad can cause a great deal of comment and bring in practically no sales. An ad may be so beautiful or clever that as far as the customer is concerned the sales message is lost.

When You Use Several Media

When your ads appear simultaneously in different media—such as the newspaper, on radio and television, in direct mail pieces, and as handbills—you should try to evaluate the relative effectiveness of each. You can check one printed medium against the other by using companion (the same or almost identical) ads in the newspaper, direct mail, and handbills.

You can make the job of analyzing and comparing results from among the media easier by varying your copy—the message. Your ad copy thus becomes the means of identifying your ad response.

You can check broadcast media—radio and TV—by slanting your message. Suppose, for example, that you advertise an item at 20 percent reduction. Your radio or TV ad might say something like this. "Come in and tell us you want this product at 20 percent off."

You can compare these responses with results from your "20 percent off" newspaper ad. Require the customer to bring in the newspaper ad—or a coupon from it.

Some of the ways to vary the copy are: a combination of the brand name with a word or some words indicating the product type; picture variations; size variations; and color variations. You might use the last three to check your printed ads against each other as well as against your radio and TV ads.

Be careful that the copy variation is not so great that a different impression is received from each medium. Here you would, in effect, have two different ads.

TWELVE

Advertising and Publicity: The Perfect Business Marriage

*Thinking Creatively / Reports, Surveys, Polls, Statistics /
Testimonials, Speeches, Appointments / Unusual Displays /
Business Trips / Calendar Events, Parades / Success Stories /
Word-of-Mouth Advertising / Conclusion*

ADVERTISING AND PUBLICITY JOIN TOGETHER IN A PERFECT business marriage of convenience if proper attention is given to each. Too often, the small business owner drops publicity when a reasonable advertising budget can be afforded—a costly and short-sighted approach. You can be sure the business giants do no such thing. Instead they mix and match publicity and advertising, getting maximum results from double exposure. When you spend a sizable amount running a full-page ad to announce a new product, doesn't it make sense to prepare a single publicity release which can double results?

The small business owner spends more time and less money producing publicity, while advertising costs more in dollars but requires less time. Integrating the two requires the timing ability of a fine performer, but once you get the hang of it, your profits will convince you the effort was worthwhile.

The most convincing reason you need continuous, planned and executed promotion—through advertising and publicity—is simple arithmetic. The National Retail Merchants Association estimates that the average store would go out of business in three or four years if it did no promotion—20 to 25 percent of customers are lost annually. These customers must be replenished by new ones if your business is to maintain the status quo.

Combining advertising and publicity is the best way to maintain the status quo while producing growth. No business outgrows its need for promotion. Those who think otherwise find themselves preparing a "going out of business" promotion through the same channels they could have used to better advantage.

Learn to turn every advertising advantage into a publicity opportunity, and vice versa, and learn to create your own ideas on which to hinge promotion. You may think yours is a business that has nothing to promote through such a combination, but if you dig deeply, you can come up with something.

For example, take Joe's Diner. The diner was one of hundreds of diners, doing the same thing all diners do. Joe was one of hundreds of owners, all doing much the same thing. What on earth could Joe do to combine publicity and advertising which could lift him above a sea of diners?

Joe had started his diner in the middle of a small-sized city and soon found himself doing a brisk business through word-of-mouth advertising and ads in the local newspaper. Soon Joe became so secure counting his future profits based on his present business that he failed to notice a new direction in his growth. Joe's Diner had become a teenage hangout—fine for Joe until the supply of teenagers began to peter out. Joe noticed that his adult customers were dropping off and some told him, bluntly, exactly why. They didn't like the loud music and the noisy teenagers.

The loss of his older customers proved to be fortunate for Joe, because it forced him to think hard about getting them back and, in doing so, he successfully combined advertising and publicity.

Joe's Diner had an advantage over other similar diners in his town since Joe served good, plain food at authentically low prices. His older customers had left reluctantly; therefore when Joe advertised a "quiet dinner hour" between 5 P.M. and 7 P.M.—substituting soft music for the blare of the juke box—he began to regain many of his old customers. Joe didn't stop here. He added a new wrinkle to his old business through advertising and publicity. He beat the competition by offering senior citizen discounts on dinners served between 5 P.M. and 6 P.M., a slow period, and he instituted a weekly two-for-one-price dinner for people over the age of 65. Added to this, Joe included an all-vegetable dinner on his menu, and a salt-free special.

Joe called up the local newspaper editor—of the paper in which his ads ran regularly—and suggested a feature story about his senior citizen discounts and menu specials. He did the same thing with the local radio station. As a result, Joe found himself on the front page of the newspaper along with a well-known elderly couple, first to take advantage of the Senior Citizen Special.

Joe could have waited—passively—for the declining teenage population to put him out of business, or he could have run his ad without any attempt to combine publicity. Instead he maximized the results of advertising and publicity by the combination. Sure, events worked in his favor. He *was* the first in town to institute senior citizen discounts which made the story more important. But next year he can add another wrinkle and get the same coverage all over again. Smart business owners do it everyday. To find out who they are, read your local newspaper and listen to your local radio station. No matter what kind of business you own, you too can create publicity and combine it with your advertising. If you think you can't, just imagine what would happen if you were able to afford the best advertising and public relations firm in the country. You can bet your last promotion dollar their creative people would find angles to your business you never thought existed. So save yourself the money and begin to think of the angles yourself.

THINKING CREATIVELY

Let's assume that you have run a catchy, clever ad in your local newspaper, and you want to get as much mileage out of it as possible. You have sent to your local newspaper and radio station press releases which were dumped into wastebaskets—always a possibility. Is there anything else you can do to maximize your promotion pulling power?

There are plenty of ways you can combine advertising and promotion which have nothing to do with the media. Promotion occurs whenever people are reached. Suppose your newspaper ad featured a coupon special you want to distribute. You can reproduce the ad and hand it out in your store, use it for posters to put up in shopping centers, tack it on bulletin boards; leave a stack in your church; pass them out on street corners; ask your business neighbors to give them out in their stores (assuming they are not competitors); leave them at the local library; include them in your direct mail; pass them out at football games; hand-deliver them door to door; and nail them on telephone poles.

There is no limit to the possibilities for combining advertising and publicity—any way your reach to customers is good if it produces profits which aren't consumed in production costs. Start dreaming up ideas in your head, jotting down the ones that seem realistic. Think of your next ad in terms of combining publicity. Create something new, something newsworthy. Here's a tried and tested idea to get you started rolling your own ideas:

Give or receive awards. How many times have you seen the line under the photograph in the newspaper: "Joe Doakes, local businessman, gives award to student with highest average in business subjects"? Awards go to the oldest person in town, the youngest, the newborn, the celebrity, the best gardener, etc.

In fact, many business owners get publicity by giving awards to their own employees. Such stories regularly make the daily newspapers with a photograph and a story.

Sports awards are also popular with business owners. And now that girls are supposed to be treated equally in sports, thousands of "new" award ideas should begin forming in the minds of thousands of business owners who want to get in on the "first" awards theme.

The award you give can be anything from a framed certificate to an expensive plaque—it won't matter. It's the recognition that counts.

REPORTS, SURVEYS, POLLS, STATISTICS

Whatever your business, there is a statistic, or a survey, that covers it. The government publishes a battery of statistics about every conceivable subject. Almanacs and record books are published by the dozens. Inside the covers is a wealth of information awaiting use in your business. Use a teaser line in your ad: "Do you know the average American consumed 135 pounds of sugar last year?" Use the ad, combining publicity, for a reducing salon, an exercise business, a health food store, a dress shop announcing the bathing-suit season, etc.

Suppose you own a chicken farm and you're selling fresh eggs. You can find a statistic telling how many million eggs are consumed each year. You can find a report revealing the age of supermarket eggs—generally about six weeks—or you can use a poll telling how many people like sunny-side-up eggs, soft-boiled, one minute or two minutes. Of course you'll want to steer clear of reports on the cholesterol content of egg yolks. In reverse exploitation, you might, however, point out the chemical additive content in the new egg substitutes, marketed to take advantage of the cholesterol scare.

People never tire of reading polls and surveys about everything under the sun. It matters not if the poll is big or little, trivial or significant. Many business owners take their own polls. Remember the livestock feed retailer who successfully predicted Truman's election in 1948 by taking his own poll? He made the prediction on the number of bags of feed he sold with a Democratic or Republican symbol. His own poll turned out to be correct when all the others were wrong, and it got him nationwide publicity—the kind that happens once in a lifetime to a small business.

Suppose you own a small business and give out campaign shopping bags with the names of the two candidates for mayor. You keep count, and ten days before election you make your predictions based on the number of bags people have chosen. If your prediction is wrong, you can always write an analysis of "What went wrong with the results I thought were in the bag."

TESTIMONIALS, SPEECHES, APPOINTMENTS

Testimonials are statements commending something—a service, a product, an action, a person. You can build your own testimonials as many small business owners do. All you need is somebody in your town to agree to the use of their name in your ads or publicity. They don't have to be well-known—although that never hurts. It can be several customers—a series run week after week. Many businesses find this a particularly good way to get new customers—the roofing company that gives a special price to a neighborhood resident in order to use the name to solicit new business; the tree surgeon who gives you a list of customers in your neighborhood. There is no better way to get new business than by pointing to satisfied customers.

When the owner of a nursery gives a speech to the local garden club, it's a good springboard to combine publicity and advertising. Think ahead and run a Garden Club Special in your ad. Give away a rare plant in a raffle to raise funds for the club. Suggest having the club meet at your nursery. Conduct a tour, give free soil tests, put out a series of garden pamphlets, announce Rose Week, give away hundred-pound bags of manure in cooperation with organic gardeners. Every owner of a small business can come up with new and different ideas to promote his or her business. The owner of a small nursery in an Eastern suburb began a very successful newspaper column on gardening which grew into a series of books.

Every community is filled with committees and every newspaper is filled with stories about their appointments. Do your civic duty, but combine it in your ads and publicity. Start your own committee. Create your own board.

UNUSUAL DISPLAYS

When you spend days setting up a unique display at your place of business, it might have wider public appeal. A dress shop displays turn-of-the-century clothing in its windows at the time the new designer clothing is strikingly familiar. It makes a clever feature story with a picture. A toy shop collects dolls from all nations. A candy store makes candy in its display window. A clock repairer features antique clocks in his window.

Begin a collection which will tie in with your business. Small business is rich in history. Anything from the village bootery to the local service station can compile a unique history of its own business "roots."

BUSINESS TRIPS

Whenever you go travelling in connection with your business, tie it in with your local publicity and advertising. Many business owners manage to get publicity by announcing that they are going and announcing what happened after their return. This is particularly effective when you attend a conference which discusses trends in your business, new products, new services.

CALENDAR EVENTS, PARADES

Labor Day, Easter, the Fourth of July, Christmas, St. Patrick's Day, Decoration Day, St. Valentine's Day—there are old and new angles every year. If you look back through a century of newspapers, you wouldn't need the date to tell you the time of year. These stories are good, standard fare. Next Valentine's Day, try putting up a 50-foot heart on top of your place of business. Will it work? Certainly it will. Try it and see.

Everybody loves a parade—especially business people whose names float down the street spelled out in rose petals. It's all good clean fun and good business at the same time. Get into the spirit and into the next parade that your town sponsors. Come up with a winner—not a run-of-the-mill entry nobody will remember past the end of the parade.

Mother's Day, Father's Day, Fire Prevention Week, Be Kind to Animals Week, Pickle Week, and Olive Day—use the ones that somebody else made up or create one of your own. Each of these special days, now so familiar, began as a germinating thought in somebody's brain. So germinate your own.

Cornerstone laying for new buildings, unveiling of statues, monuments, tablets—all provide opportunity for the business with a tie-in—building supply retailers, real estate businesses, sculptures, those serving on committees planning events.

Each town or community has its own unique events around which business can build advertising and publicity. It can be something as unusual as the Ramp Festival in West Virginia or as usual as a Chamber of Commerce picnic in Wyoming. The important thing is for you to link these events to opportunities for advertising and publicity. Be tasteful in your selection and don't turn into a publicity hound, defeating your own purpose. Carefully select those events which will be good for you and for the community.

Keep a file of regular community events in which you participate. After a few years you will have built your own anniversary story: "the seventh consecutive year," the "eighth annual event." A file will show you at a glance what worked and what didn't.

SUCCESS STORIES

Nothing succeeds like success. Success is a great subject for advertising and publicity and builds on itself. What does it really mean when McDonald's informs you it has sold a trillion hamburgers and opened a hundred new franchises? It is success that is being ballyhooed.

Get aboard with your success story. Business newspapers love success stories. Your business volume is up, employment is up, expansion is planned, you're outgrowing your old location, you've had the best Christmas ever, you expect the best summer season.

WORD-OF-MOUTH ADVERTISING

There's a small counter-type grill in Marathon, Fla., which depends upon word-of-mouth advertising except in rare instances. It does a land-office business with people lining up three deep for a turn at the plain counter. What's the appeal? An enormous grouper (fish) sandwich which sells for $1.25 and a steak, grouper, or shrimp dinner, fit for a hungry truck driver, for well under $3.00. The grill has built a brisk business on word-of-mouth tributes and 99-percent return business. Almost every customer comes back.

This grill, aside from having simple customer traffic needs, is the exception, not the rule. Word-of-mouth advertising is nice—even critical—but you can't count on it to make your business grow. It is unpredictable and unreliable. You need steady, week-by-week recognition to build and stabilize a business.

CONCLUSION

L. T. White was a businessman who began his career as a meter reader and became vice-president and director of research and education for a large corporation. His wit, wisdom, and home-spun philosophy made him a successful lecturer on his favorite subject—business.

White conducted research among small business owners by moving into a community during his research. Perhaps that's the reason his advice is so realistic and down-to-earth. He knew what he was talking about firsthand.

When you are considering your advertising and publicity, keep L. T. White's advice in mind:

- Never suggest a purchase you can't *prove* is needed.
- Never criticize what the buyer is using—he (she) picked it.
- People buy benefits, not products.
- People have four buying motives:
     To live.
     To learn.
     To love.
     To laugh.
- Business is the activity of helping people through selling.
- If you want to earn more, learn more.

The management of a small business combines the world's most interesting subject, human behavior, with a ready-built laboratory. A multitude of people agree. In fact, in this country:

- There are 9.4 million small businesses.
- Small business accounts for 43 percent of the country's gross national product.
- Small business provides more than 52 percent of the country's total employment.
- Small business provides—directly or indirectly—a livelihood for 100 million Americans.

Small business is a tremendous force. The economic health of the country depends upon the success of small business people—individuals who take the personal and financial risks of betting on themselves. The free-enterprise system—the risk of making it big or going broke—has built this nation. It's the juice that keeps hopes alive. So get in there and succeed.

The bigger you get, the more badly-needed jobs you will create.

As you build and strive and grow, let the world know about your success. Beat your own drum by becoming a lifetime member of the BBBP Club: Build a Better Business through Promotion—advertising promotion and promotion through publicity.

Suggested Reading

Arnold, Edmund C., *Profitable Newspaper Advertising* (New York: Harper & Row, 1960).

Bloomenthal, Howard, *Promoting Your Cause* (New York: Funk & Wagnalls, 1971).

Caples, John, *Making Ads Pay* (New York: Dover, 1957).

Cook, Harvey R., *More Profits Through Advertising* (New York: Drake, 1969).

Doyle, Dennis M., *Efficient Accounting and Record-Keeping* (New York: Wiley, 1977).

Fehlman, Frank E., *How to Write Advertising Copy That Sells* (New York: Funk & Wagnalls, 1950).

Fulweller, John H., *How to Promote Your Shopping Center* (New York: Chain Store Age Books, 1973).

Gellerman, Saul W., *The Management of Human Relations* (New York: Holt, Rinehart & Winston, 1966).

Halley, William C., *Employee Publications* (Radnor, Pa.: Chilton, 1959).

Heyel, Carl, *Organizing Your Job in Management* (New York: American Management Assn., 1960).

Karch, R. Randolph, and Edward J. Buber, *Graphic Arts Procedures* (Chicago: American Technical Society, 1967).

Krentzman, Harvey C., *Managing For Profits* (Washington, D.C.: U.S. Small Business Administration, 1968).

Lewis, H. Gordon, *How to Handle Your Own Public Relations* (Chicago: Nelson Hall, 1976).

Lewis, Herschell G., *The Businessman's Guide to Advertising and Sales Promotion* (New York: McGraw-Hill, 1976).

Loffel, Egon W., *Financing Your Business* (New York: Wiley, 1977).

Luick, John P., and William L. Siegler, *Sales Promotion and Modern Merchandising* (New York: McGraw-Hill, 1968).

Malickson, David L., and John W. Nason, *Advertising—How to Write the Kind That Works* (New York: Scribner's, 1977).

Reeves, Rosser, *Reality in Advertising* (New York: Knopf, 1961).

Scholz, William, *Communications in the Business Organization* (Englewood Cliffs, N.J.: Prentice-Hall, 1966).

Seder, John W., *Credit and Collections* (New York: Wiley, 1977).

Smith, Cynthia S., *How to Get Big Results from a Small Advertising Budget* (New York: Hawthorn, 1973).

Stevenson, George A., *Graphic Arts Encyclopedia* (New York: McGraw-Hill, 1968).

Weiner, Richard, *Professional Guide to Public Relations Service* (Englewood Cliffs, N.J.: Prentice-Hall, 1968).

INDEX

5-23